A WOMAN'S GUIDE

To Fixing The Car

A WOMAN'S GUIDE
To Fixing The Car

Paul and Arleen Weissler

WALKER AND COMPANY • New York

The authors wish to thank the public relations departments of Chrysler Corporation and General Motors for many of the illustrations in Chapter 1, and Bernard L. Price for several pieces of original artwork in that chapter.

First published in the United States of America in 1973 by the Walker Publishing Company, Inc.

Published simultaneously in Canada by Fitzhenry & Whiteside, Limited, Toronto.

ISBN: 0-8027-0416-6

Library of Congress Catalog Card Number: 72-95786

Printed in the United States of America.

10 9 8 7 6 5 4 3 2 1

*To Pauline Gerard, Belle Lovinger and Betty Slatin—
three of the many women we hope will find this book
helpful in taking the mystery out of automobile repair.*

Contents

Introduction

IF you're a woman who owns a car, sexual discrimination probably is costing you money. It is a fact of life that most drivers—both men and women—know very little about the operation of their cars. When the car breaks down, both are at the mercy of the repair shop. But here is where the equality ends. Since most mechanics believe that a man *may* know something about automobiles, while a woman surely does *not,* the man gets a far better shake every time.

There are several reasons why you take on second-class citizenship every time you enter a garage. First, it is traditionally a man's world and, like many women, you probably feel uncomfortable and out of place in it. This apparent discomfort leaves you an open target for being soft-soaped into buying things you do not need at some types of shops. Although most shops are honest, the cheats that do exist are more likely to try to take advantage of a woman than a man. Secondly, since it is assumed that you know nothing about a car, you will frequently hear even at honest shops, "Just leave the car, lady; we'll take care of it. Call us later and we'll tell you what the job cost." A man is far more likely to be told what the problem is and be given a choice of repair options, allowing him to make the cost-value decisions that fit his wallet.

To get an even break, you must know something about car repair and be able to communicate your automotive savvy by asking intelligent questions and providing useful information on your car's problems.

There is nothing mysterious about an automobile. Nor

is there any sex link to understanding it. You don't have to become a mechanic to comprehend the options open to you.

Begin by reading your car owner's manual. It won't be of much help in making decisions about repair, but it can give you an idea of what periodic maintenance is necessary. If you keep a car well maintained you will have fewer repair problems. If you buy more maintenance than the car needs, however, you will waste money.

This book is intended to pick up where the owner's manual stops, to help you get more than an even break. It will give you the basic know-how you need to get the right job at the right price and, if you wish, to do some basic maintenance yourself. With little effort, you can know a lot more about a car than all but a handful of men, and you can get the fair treatment you want.

A WOMAN'S GUIDE

To Fixing The Car

CHAPTER 1 | How Your Car Works and When It Doesn't

Anyone of average intelligence can comprehend the basics of a car's operation. After all, how many geniuses have you ever met working as mechanics?

A car is a machine. Because it must do so many things, however, it must use a wide variety of devices and systems. Taken together, they form a complex operation. Individually, they are simple, and if you are familiar with the principles behind such devices as a bicycle, egg beater and perfume atomizer, you can understand how a car works.

You only have to overcome any mental block you may have regarding machinery. An automobile has a lot of this-connects-to-this-which-connects-to-that about it, but if you go slowly and give the material in this chapter a try, you'll find you can handle it.

This chapter is not intended to tell you how a mechanic works. You don't need to know *how* to fix something, you just must understand *what* it is that needs to be fixed. Your first step, therefore, is to acquire an understanding of how each system works, and what usually goes wrong. This information will enable you to deal with a repair shop on an intelligent basis, and will help you know when unnecessary work is being proposed.

Here is an overall look at the operation of a car, *See Fig. 1.*

Until 1912, the car was started by the driver turning a handle inserted into the engine. This was replaced by the electric starter, a small motor bolted to the engine.

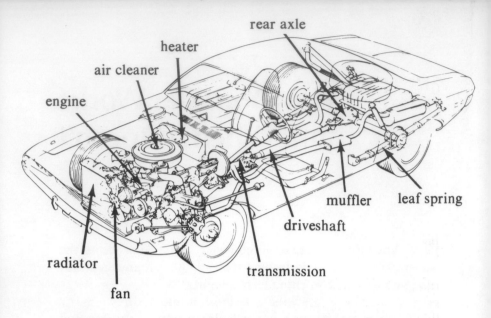

engine • air cleaner • heater • rear axle • muffler • leaf spring • driveshaft • radiator • fan • transmission

Fig. 1. *Don't let this phantom view of the innards of a car scare you. If you concentrate on one system at a time, learning how it operates, everything will fall into place in your mind.*

The electricity to operate the starter, lights and other accessories is supplied by the battery. The battery is kept charged by a generator, a device turned by the engine to create electrical current.

The automobile develops power in the engine, using fuel delivered from the gas tank by the fuel system, and exploding it with sparks from the ignition system. Excess heat developed by the engine is carried away by the cooling system. The burned gases are expelled into the exhaust system.

The power developed by the engine must be transferred to the wheels in order to make the car go. In most cars, the power is transferred to the rear wheels, in some to the front wheels (called front-wheel drive) and in a few, such as Jeeps and tow trucks, to all four wheels (called four-wheel drive). Every car has four wheels, but if power is transferred to either pair, the other pair will roll along too. Four-wheel drive provides the best traction, but it is expensive to produce and only specialty vehicles that need it get it.

The power transfer goes through several components (called, collectively, the drive train). The first step from the engine is the clutch (on cars with manual transmission) or torque converter (on cars with automatic transmission), which permits the engine to disconnect from the drive train when the car is stopped. This allows the engine to keep running without moving the car.

The power continues into the transmission, where gears are selected (manually by the driver in a standard transmission, partially automatically in an automatic transmission). Certain gears permit the car to be moved away from a stopped position, others permit cruising speeds.

In the conventional car, power leaves the transmission by a long shaft to the rear, where it goes into the rear axle assembly.

The rear axle is also a transmission in that it contains gears, although no selection is possible in a passenger car. The gears in the rear axle change the direction of the power and transmit it through a short shaft to each rear wheel. The rear wheels spin and the car moves.

The brake system stops the car. When you step on the brake pedal, you are indirectly applying a frictional force to parts bolted to the four wheels.

Now let's see how each of these systems, and some others, including suspension and steering, actually work.

ENGINE

An automobile engine produces power by burning a mixture of gasoline and air in a small space called a combustion chamber. When this mixture burns, it expands and pushes out in every possible direction.

In the car engine, *See Fig. 2,* the combustion chamber is located just above a cylinder, into which is installed a closely fitting plug called a piston. The piston is capable of being moved up and down in the cylinder.

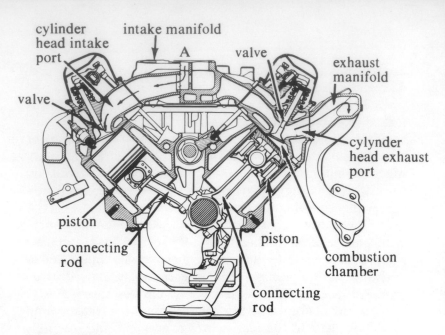

Fig. 2. *This is a cut-away view of a V-8 engine from the front. When an engine is drawn this way, you can see only one of the two valves that are in each combustion chamber. The one on the left is an intake valve, which, when it opens, admits the air-fuel mixture. The one on the right is an exhaust valve, which allows burned gases to flow into the exhaust manifold (the piping that begins the exhaust system). The piston on the right is at the top of its stroke, and has squeezed the fuel mixture into the tiny space above it called the combustion chamber. An instantaneous spark will set the mixture ablaze, forcing the piston down (creating power). When the piston rises, the exhaust valve will open, and the burned gases will be forced into the exhaust system. If all this is mind-boggling, come back to it later, when some of the other illustrations have clarified things for you.*

When the piston is lowered in a running engine, it creates a vacuum in the cylinder and draws in a mixture of fuel and air. The piston is then pushed up to the top of the cylinder, compressing the air-fuel charge. A spark ignites the mixture, which expands and pushes the piston downward.

The greater the compression of the air-fuel charge, the greater the expansion during combustion and, because the expansion is power, the greater the power that is developed. The term "compression ratio" relates to the amount of compression. High-compression engines develop more power than those of equal size but lower compression.

The downward force on the piston is power, but since the automobile needs rotary motion, a conversion must be made.

Converting the downward movement of the piston to rotary power is simple: a rod connects the piston to a shaft (called a crankshaft), *See Figs. 3 and 4*. To understand this, just look at a bicycle, and visualize the movement of your leg and the bike's mechanism. As you pedal, your leg moves up and down (applying power on the downstroke, just as the force of burning gas on a piston), but the placement of pedals at the ends of the shaft makes your foot go around in a circle.

You know that your car has four, six, or eight cylinders (twelve in some European sports cars). The bicycle is the equivalent of the one cylinder engine. Just visualize a bicycle with a very wide seat and a shaft that has been extended to accommodate six sets of pedals for six riders. This should give you the idea of many pistons applying power to a single shaft.

Unlike the bicycle, cylinders with pistons can be ar-

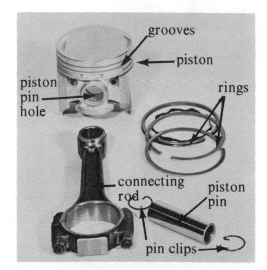

Fig. 3. *Here's a close look at the piston and rod assembly. There are three grooves in the piston and three rings that fit in them (one of the rings has that corrugated metal spacer behind it). The piston pin goes into the hole in the side of the piston, then through the top hole in the rod, and then through another hole on the opposite side of the piston. Two clips hold the pin in place, so the rod can swivel on the pin while the pin itself is held in place.*

grooves

piston

piston pin hole

rings

connecting rod

piston pin

pin clips

Fig. 4. *This is the crankshaft, which takes the up-and-down movement of the pistons and converts it to rotary motion, something like the action in a carousel. The smooth, round, shiny surfaces are called journals. Those labeled "A" are in line with the centerline of the crankshaft and are called main bearing journals. Those labeled "B" are offset and are called crankpin or connecting rod journals because the lower end of the connecting rod is wrapped around them. The big triangular-shaped pieces on the crankshaft are called counterweights and their purpose is to help smooth out the rotary motion of the crankshaft.*

ranged in other than a straight line, and the most popular arrangement is the V-8, in which four cylinders are in line along each side of an engine shaped like the letter "V," *See Fig. 6.* This layout allows more power-producing cylinders and pistons in an engine compartment of moderate size.

Regardless of whether the engine has the pistons all in line or in sections of a V-design (each section called a "bank"), the rods all connect to a single crankshaft.

Why many cylinders instead of a small number of larger ones? The reason is that the power impulses from the downward movements of the pistons are not individually smooth, but when there are many impulses, the rotary motion of the crankshaft is made relatively smooth.

Another major contributor to engine smoothness is the heavy wheel at the rear end of the crankshaft, called the flywheel, *See Fig. 5.* The flywheel sustains momentum,

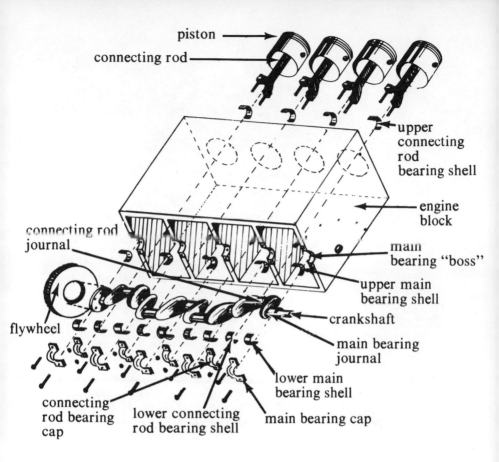

Fig. 5. *Here's a drawing to make things clearer. Notice the curved surfaces in the bottom of the engine block. They're called bearing bosses and they hold the upper main bearing shell. Then observe the main bearing cap and its curved surface, which holds the lower shell. Move the crankshaft up into the main bearing bosses (with the shells in place), then bolt on the caps. The bearing shells provide a super-smooth surface for the super-smooth crankshaft journals, and when a little oil is pumped in, the crankshaft can rotate on these bearings with negligible wear. Take a new look at the connecting rods. This type has projecting threaded studs, just like those in Fig. 3. There are upper and lower bearing shells, the upper fitting into the rod, the lower into the rod cap. Nuts are threaded onto the studs and the assembly clamps around the connecting rod journal of the crankshaft, which because it is offset, will push the rod (and piston) up and pull it down as it rotates in the main bearings.*

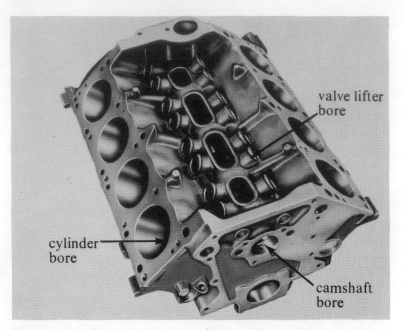

valve lifter bore

cylinder bore

camshaft bore

Fig. 6. *Here's a real V-8 engine block with everything out. You can see the eight cylinders, plus the hole into which the camshaft fits, and one of the many holes for the valve lifters. If you look carefully, you can see that the camshaft is in perfect position when installed to operate the valve lifters. Engineers and mechanics call all these holes "bores."*

somewhat like the blades of a fan that continue to turn after you've turned it off.

Not all of the power produced by the engine is sent to the wheels. Some of the power of a spinning crankshaft can be used to operate other components within the engine and attached to it. The simplest way to utilize this power is to bolt a gear and a pulley onto the front end of the crankshaft and join these with other gears and pulleys.

A gear, *See Fig. 7,* is a circular part with teeth and the simple egg beater offers an example of how it works. When you turn the handle of an egg beater (a form of hand-operated crankshaft), a gear turns. The teeth of this gear mesh with the teeth of another gear which is in turn attached to the beaters and spins them.

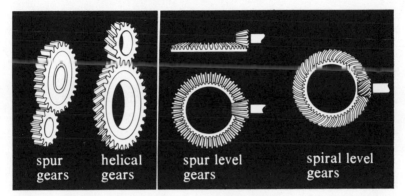

spur gears   helical gears   spur level gears   spiral level gears

Fig. 7. *There are many different types of gears. The way the teeth are cut distingushes them and determines the names. The spur gear is the type normally used for crankshaft and camshaft gears. When quieter operation is necessary, the helical design is used. Bevel gears, which make the motion turn a corner, are used in rear axles.*

In an automobile engine, the crankshaft gear meshes with the gear of another shaft called the camshaft, *See Fig. 8.* In most cases, the gears do not actually mesh, but a special chain (called the timing chain) is wrapped around them, effectively joining them. The bicycle chain drive, in which a gear at the pedal crank mechanism drives another gear at the rear wheel, is an example of this kind of joining.

The pulley is a gear without teeth. Instead, it has an edge groove into which a large, not-very-elastic rubber band fits. This band, called a belt, is wrapped around a second and perhaps even a third pulley, *See Fig. 9.* At least one of the pulleys can be moved and locked in any of a range of

Fig. 8. *The crankshaft drives the camshaft by means of a gear at the end of each shaft and a chain—called the timing chain—around both of them. These gears and the chain are at the front of the engine, covered by a sheet metal piece called the timing chain cover that keeps the oil which lubricates them from leaking out.*

positions, so the belt around all the pulleys is tight. When the crankshaft pulley is turned by the crankshaft, the tight belt also spins any other pulleys around which it is wound, just as a clothesline wrapped around pulleys, an example with which you may be familiar. These other pulleys may operate a generator, power steering pump, cooling system water pump or the compressor in an air conditioning system.

Our engine now has pistons that move up and down in cylinders, and gears and pulleys to operate some of the engine's systems.

CUBIC INCH DISPLACEMENT AND ENGINE PERFORMANCE

The term "cubic inch displacement of the engine" is one you have probably heard. The meaning of the term and the particular number that applies to your engine are valuable information, both for the mechanic who works on it and for you if you choose to do some maintenance yourself.

The term is a measurement of engine size or, more accurately, the total volume of all the cylinders—from the top surface of each piston (when it is at its lowest position in the cylinder) to the top of the combustion chamber.

The larger or longer the cylinders, the greater the number of cubic inches, the more air-fuel mixture they can hold and burn, and the greater the amount of power they produce—in theory, that is.

As a practical matter, the total number of cubic inches is only one factor in engine performance. Also important are the compression ratio (the measurement of how much the air-fuel mixture is squeezed before ig-

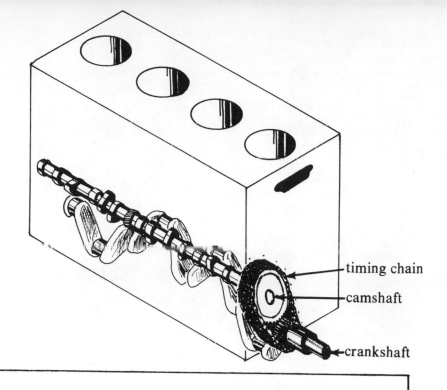

timing chain
camshaft
crankshaft

nition) and the design of the camshaft (which determines when the valves open—if the intake valve opens earlier, more air-fuel mixture can be admitted, as an example). Still a third factor is how fast the engine is capable of rotating, and there are many engineering design factors that go into that.

The cubic inch displacement, however, is a standard reference term, particularly when ordering parts for an engine. Most catalogs will reference a part number for a specific displacement engine, and there is often no other identification than make and model of car. Inasmuch as a given model can come with many engines of similar type (six or V-8), finding out which engine you have can be important.

The number may be embossed on an emblem on the air cleaner cover, or on a valve cover, or perhaps even on a fender ornament. If not, call the zone office of the car manufacturer and ask to have it checked for you. If you give the office certain numbers on the car's identification plate, it can determine the displacement by reference to engine code bulletins it has.

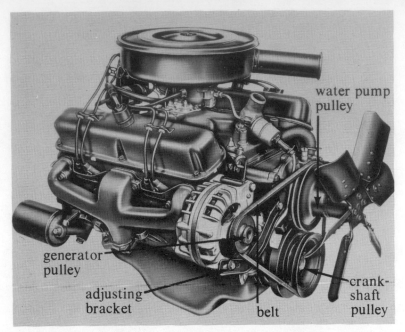

Fig. 9. *The grooved circular parts are pulleys—gears without teeth. A belt tightly fitted around them transfers power from the crankshaft to such units as the generator and water pump. Additional belts and pulleys are used to drive air conditioning compressors and power steering pumps. Note the adjusting bracket on the generator. Its elongated hole permits pivoting the generator outward as necessary to apply tension to the belt. At the appropriate point along the elongated hole, the mounting bolt is tightened. Proper belt tension is necessary to transfer power from the crankshaft pulley.*

    Most of the engine's systems are driven by the camshaft. Why is it necessary to have this second shaft when the original source of power is the crankshaft? The answer is that the crankshaft is at the bottom of the engine and its location is inconvenient for most engine systems. Positioning the camshaft at or near the top of the engine provides advantages in the layout of components.

    The camshaft is the controlling unit for the following: the valves that admit the fuel mixture into the combustion chambers; the valves that allow the burned gases to pass into the exhaust system; the ignition distributor that routes the sparks to burn the fuel mixtures; the fuel pump that draws gasoline from the tank; and the oil pump that supplies lubrication for the engine's internal working parts.

A typical camshaft, *See Fig. 10,* has gears and teardrop-shaped projections called "cams" (from which it derives its name). The cams operate the valves, usually by means of a linkage system.

At this point, let's complete the combustion chamber. Visualize a sink with two stoppers and a third hole for the

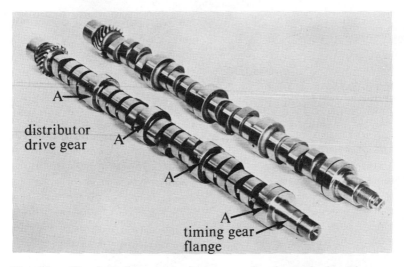

distributor drive gear

timing gear flange

Fig. 10. *Here's a close-up look at a couple of camshafts. The parts labeled "A" are journals and, like crankshaft journals, are super-smooth surfaces which rotate in bearings. Unlike crankshaft bearings, the camshaft bearings are not usually made in half shells, (simply because the camshaft is installed differently) but in whole circles. The "timing gear flange" at the front is where the gear around which the timing chain is wrapped is fitted (see Fig. 8). The distributor drive gear at the rear is actually part of the camshaft. It operates both the ignition distributor and the engine oil pump. The teardrop-shaped protrusions, of course, are the cams, and their job is to push on the valve lifters to open the valves in the combustion chamber. When the high spot of the cam comes up, it pushes on the valve lifter. As the cam rotates, its shape permits the lifter to drop, and a spring pushes the valve closed.*

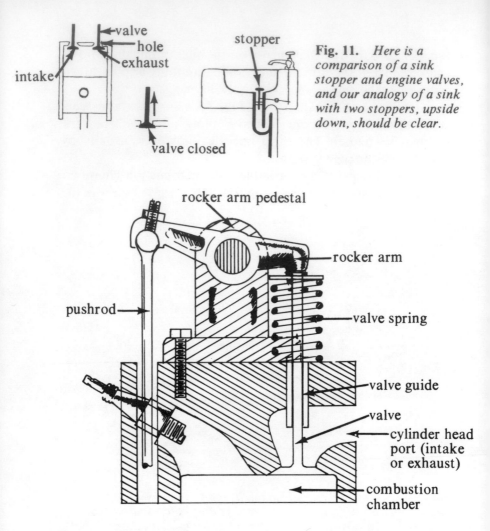

intake — valve — hole — exhaust

valve closed

stopper

Fig. 11. *Here is a comparison of a sink stopper and engine valves, and our analogy of a sink with two stoppers, upside down, should be clear.*

rocker arm pedestal

rocker arm

pushrod

valve spring

valve guide

valve

cylinder head port (intake or exhaust)

combustion chamber

Fig. 12. *This drawing should make the operation of the valve train a bit clearer. The camshaft pushes up on the valve lifter (both parts not shown) and the valve lifter pushes up on the pushrod. The upward movement of the pushrod pivots the rocker, which pushes down on the valve stem against spring pressure to open the valve. When the valve opens, the cylinder head port is open to the combustion chamber and either a fuel mixture flows in or an exhaust gas flows out, depending on whether it's an intake port or an exhaust port. The camshaft continues to turn and the lifter drops, allowing the pushrod to drop. The valve spring unwinds and pulls the valve to which it is attached firmly closed. The engine is designed so that each valve opens and closes at exactly the right time, and the spark arrives at the plug at just the proper instant.*

device that fires the fuel mixture—the spark plug. Turn it upside down and place it over the top of the cylinder, and you've got the basics.

To understand valve action, look at the linkage arrangement that opens and closes the stopper and you'll see three parts: a long rod that you push or pull to open or close the stopper, a pivoting rod that connects the long rod to the stopper's stem, and the stopper itself, *See Figs. 11 and 12.*

The sink stopper must be pushed to open and pulled to close. If we attach a spring to the stopper stem, it will close as soon as the pushing pressure on the long rod is released.

Once we do this to both stoppers in our imaginary sink, we actually have something very close to the valve system used in an automobile engine. The spinning camshaft's teardrop-shaped cams push on the handle of the long rod (the handle is a separate part called a valve lifter; and the long rod is called a pushrod). The pivoting rod that connects the pushrod to the stopper stem is called a "rocker arm," and the stopper is called a valve. The round insert against which the stopper or valve closes is called a seat.

Each combustion chamber needs two valve linkage arrangements, one to admit the air-gasoline mixture (called the intake valve), and another to allow the burned gases to pass into the exhaust system (called the exhaust valve) *See Fig. 13.*

The cams on the camshaft push open the valves for each combustion chamber and allow them to spring closed at just the right time.

For convenience in manufacture, engines are normally built in two major parts, the cylinder head and the block, *See Fig. 14.* The cylinder head is the part into which the combustion chambers are cast. The valves are in the cylinder head, as are the springs that allow the valves to shut and the rocker arms that push the valves open. In some engine designs, the camshaft is mounted in the top of the cylinder head and pushrods and rocker arms may be eliminated.

The block contains the cylinders, crankshaft and pis-

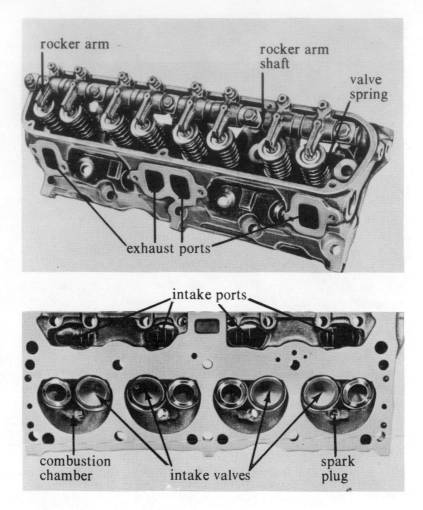

rocker arm

rocker arm
shaft

valve
spring

exhaust ports

intake ports

combustion
chamber

intake valves

spark
plug

Fig. 13.   *Here is a cylinder head from a V-8 engine with all the parts labeled. The top photo shows the ports that lead to the exhaust valves. The bottom photo (head upside down) shows the intake ports. There are four cylinders in each bank of a V-8, four intake valves and four exhaust valves, and a port for each. The intake valves are the larger ones, so a maximum amount of air-fuel mixture can be admitted. Getting rid of the exhaust is less of a problem than getting the fuel mixture in, so the exhaust valves can be made smaller.*

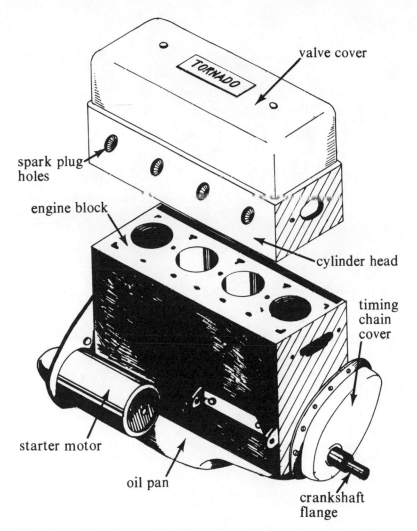

spark plug holes

engine block

valve cover

cylinder head

timing chain cover

starter motor

oil pan

crankshaft flange

Fig. 14. *A basic overall look at the engine's main sections. For convenience in manufacture, an engine has two basic sections: cylinder head and block, plus three sheet metal covers; valve covers, timing chain cover and oil pan (also called crankcase). The crankshaft flange that you see projecting from the timing chain cover is a piece on which the crankshaft pulley is mounted. Also note the position of the starter motor at the rear. It will help clarify your understanding of the starting system later in this chapter.*

Fig. 15. *Here's an upside-down view of an engine block with just the main bearing caps in place; this particular engine has five of them. You can see the smooth round holes they form and should be able to mentally drop a crankshaft right into place.*

tons, and their connecting rods. In most engines it also houses the camshaft.

An engine would not operate very long if not for an important type of part called a bearing, and a fluid, oil.

A bearing is a super-smooth ring that supports any type of moving part. In the engine, there are many bearings, the most important being the crankshaft main bearing and the piston connecting rod bearing. These bearings are made in two half-moon pieces for ease of installation. Figs. 5 and 15 show how the bearings fit in place and the smooth round surfaces—called journals—they bear against. The engine has a connecting rod bearing for each cylinder and three to seven main bearings.

Although these bearings are smooth and in contact with smooth journal surfaces on the shafts they support, lubrication is still a must to minimize friction. An oil pump, operated by a gear off the camshaft, circulates oil throughout the engine, pumping it to bearings that support connecting rods, crankshaft, and camshaft, *See Figs. 16A and B.* It also pumps oil to the valve lifters, most of which rely on oil pressure to function smoothly. As oil leaves the connecting rod bearings, it splashes up onto each cylinder, lubricating it.

The engine is basically completed by three sheet metal covers: one at the bottom of the engine (called the oil pan), one at the top (called the valve cover or rocker cover), and one at the front of the engine to cover the timing chain (called the timing chain cover).

An engine must seal in oil and (in most cases) water, and it must separate some of the different systems within. The methods of sealing vary according to what must be sealed in, how much pressure must be contained, and other similar requirements, but because sealing failures are responsible for many engine problems, you should be familiar with them.

A common type of seal is the gasket, which is placed between two flat surfaces of parts that will be bolted to-

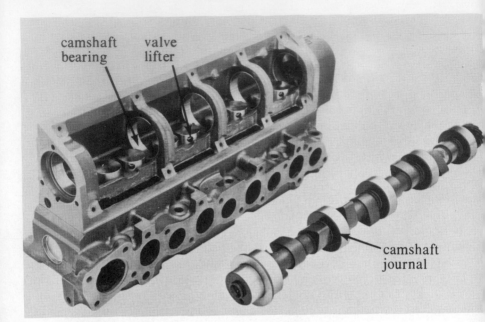

camshaft bearing   valve lifter

camshaft journal

Fig. 16A

Fig. 16. A *Take a look at an overhead camshaft engine's cylinder head. There's no pushrod or rocker in this design, just the camshaft pushing on the valve lifter. Under the valve lifter is the valve spring and valve (see Fig. 16B). Clearly this design eliminates some parts, but it takes a very long chain from the crankshaft to reach the camshaft. This particular engine, a Chevrolet Vega, has a "chain" made of stretch-resistant rubber—actually, a belt with teeth that mesh with the crankshaft and camshaft gears. A large number of imported cars have overhead camshaft engines.*

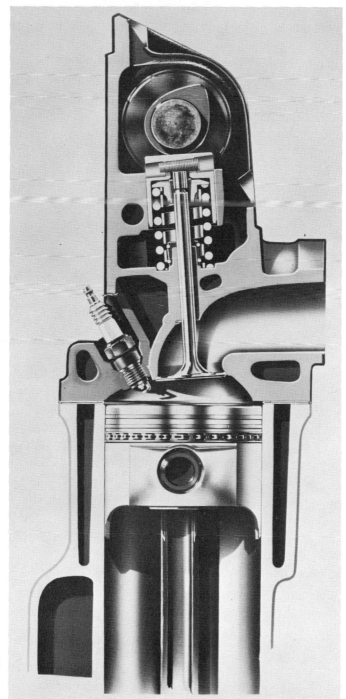

Fig. 16B

gether, *See Fig. 17*. Made of cork, rubber, treated paper, asbestos or soft metal, the gasket fills in minor irregularities in the flat surfaces when the parts are joined. Gaskets are used between the cylinder head and block (cylinder head gasket), between the oil pan and block (oil pan gasket), valve cover and cylinder head (valve cover gasket) and timing chain cover and engine block (timing cover gasket), to give only some examples among more than a dozen locations on the engine, *See Fig. 18*.

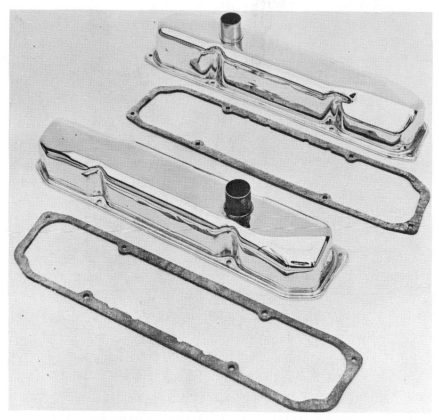

Fig. 17.   *The valve cover relies on the cork gasket below it to seal against oil leaks.*

Another seal is the rubber ring, which is used on valve stems to keep oil from dripping into the combustion chambers, *See Fig. 19.*

Perhaps the best-known seal is the piston ring. Each piston has at least three of these rings. The top two seal off the top of the cylinder and combustion chamber, to keep the compressed air-fuel mixture from getting out of the combustion chamber. A third, near the bottom of the piston, keeps oil from splashing up into the combustion chamber.

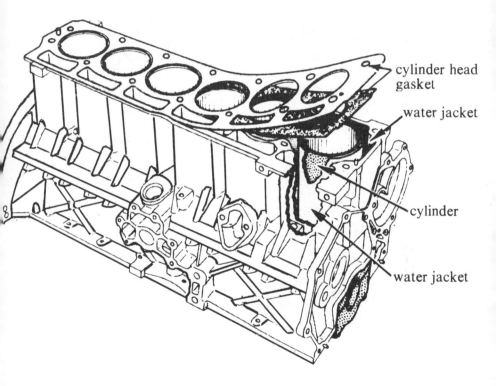

cylinder head gasket

water jacket

cylinder

water jacket

Fig. 18. *The cylinder head gasket is placed between the head and block and performs many sealing functions. It keeps the water in its passages, the oil in its passages, the compressed air-fuel mixture in the combustion chamber and the burned exhaust gases from going anywhere but into the exhaust system.*

THE WANKEL ROTARY ENGINE

The piston engine converts the up-and-down motion of pistons into rotary motion at the crankshaft. The Wankel rotary engine uses a chamber with a triangular rotor inside instead of pistons and cylinders.

Air-fuel explosions in the chamber push the rotor in a somewhat eccentric but basically rotary direction, and this motion is transferred through a gear and cam arrangement to a shaft.

Instead of valves, there are intake and exhaust ports drilled into the chamber, eliminating also the need for pushrods and lifters.

The simplified design of the Wankel engine makes it a candidate for a bright future. In the meantime, however, virtually all cars have piston engines and this chapter limits itself to the details of their operation.

What Goes Wrong

An engine normally gives little trouble for many tens of thousands of miles, provided it gets a fresh supply of engine oil and a new oil filter (which keeps the oil clean) two to four times a year. Most troubles associated with the engine are actually in contributing systems, such as the ignition or fuel systems.

The most common engine-only problems are oil leaks —from the oil pan, valve cover or timing cover gaskets. An oil leak of the drip-drop variety should not be cause for panic, so long as you add oil to prevent the engine from running low enough on lubricant to cause a major failure. The oil leak should be corrected as soon as possible, however, for it will eventually get to the point where the engine could be ruined by a rapid loss of oil. If caught at an early stage,

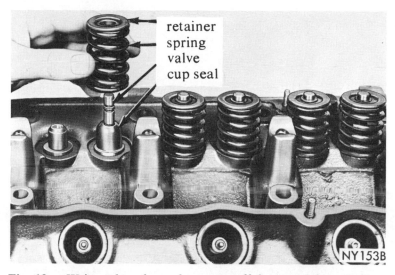

retainer
spring
valve
cup seal

NY153B

Fig. 19. *We've taken the rocker arms off the top of this cylinder head and disengaged the spring from the valve stem so you can see where the valve stem oil seals are. The valve stems ride in narrow cylinders called guides (to keep them from wobbling) and the seals keep the oil that is pumped to the top of the engine to lubricate the rocker arms from getting past the guides into the combustion chambers. The cup seal you see is only one possible design; there are many other shapes.*

some oil leaks at gasket joints can be cured by simply tightening some nuts or bolts.

Worn piston rings cause both a loss of power and increased slippage of oil into the combustion chamber, where it is burned. All engines burn some oil (a quart every 700 to 2000 miles is normal), and you should not be panicked into an engine overhaul. Defective valve stem oil seals can also cause increased oil consumption, and these seals can be changed in less than two hours on most cars, *See Fig. 19.*

A mechanic can easily check to see if the piston rings are a problem with a "compression gauge," a device that measures pressures in the cylinders, *See Fig. 20.* Low compression readings (indicating that some of the compressed air-fuel charge is being lost before burning) can be caused by worn piston rings, failure of the valves to close completely (a` less expensive problem), or rupture of the cylinder head gasket (even less expensive). There are standard techniques for determining the exact cause of low compression readings.

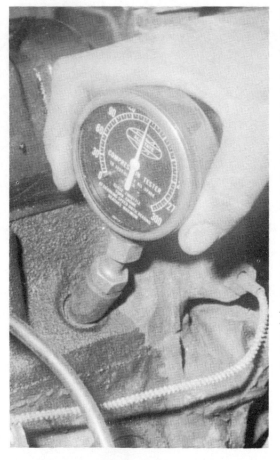

Fig. 20. *This is a compression gauge. The mechanic removes the spark plugs, holds the gauge in a spark plug hole and cranks the engine with the starter. The pressure recorded on this gauge tells him if the combustion chamber is holding in the air-fuel mixture when the piston compresses it. Leakage of the mixture reduces the pressure, and this reduces the force of the ignition explosion. Poor compression gauge readings have several causes, and the mechanic has standard techniques to isolate the problem. Today many shops have electronic testers called oscilloscopes, which often eliminate the need for use of this gauge.*

In many cases, oil consumption caused by worn piston rings can be reduced to acceptable levels by use of an oil-thickening additive, such as "STP," "Stud," "Casite Motor Honey" and DuPont oil treatment. By thickening the oil, these additives can help keep it from slipping past the rings. Also, they help the rings to seal somewhat better, improving compression. These additives are not cure-alls, however. They are merely postponers, which might, for instance, keep the engine in an older car performing acceptably until you are ready to dispose of it. Note: only one can of this additive should be used in winter, or the oil will be so thick that engine starting may be impeded.

Worn engine bearings are another possible engine malfunction, but one that prudent car owners avoid by regular engine oil and filter changes that keep the engine clean. Careful owners also eliminate the other cause of bearing failure: abuse. Avoiding high speeds with a cold engine for seven miles in warm weather, fifteen in cold weather, allows the oil to warm up and circulate freely. Keeping the engine in good tune (ignition and fuel systems adjusted periodically and new ignition parts periodically installed) also helps, for this reduces wear on the bearings by promoting smoother combustion.

Another possible source of internal engine trouble is the hydraulic valve lifter, *See Fig. 21,* used on virtually all American cars. As you recall, the valve lifter is the "handle" of the valve train, being pushed up by the camshaft. To provide shock-free operation, the typical American car has valve lifters of the hydraulic type, which are special designs that rely on clean engine oil to operate ("hydraulic" means fluid, and the fluid in this case is engine oil).

The internal parts of the hydraulic valve lifter are affected by dirt, rust and sludge in the engine oil, and if these are present in sufficient quantity, they can cause the lifter to stick or otherwise malfunction.

A lifter that doesn't operate properly will not open and close the intake and exhaust valves according to the precise schedule necessary for smooth engine performance. Most

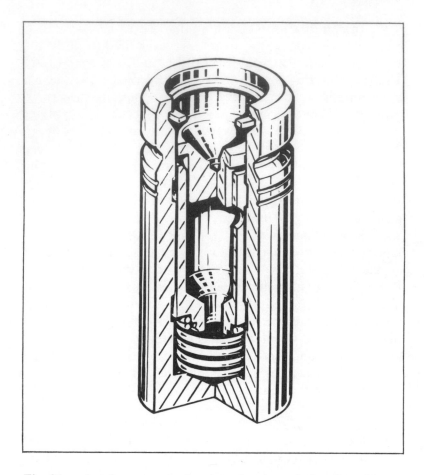

Fig. 21. *Another cutaway drawing, showing a hydraulic valve lifter—a valve lifter that works with engine oil. A V-8 has 16 of these lifters, and if the engine oil isn't changed at reasonable intervals, contaminants in dirty oil will cause them to stick. This results in engine tapping sounds and engine misfiring, and the cost of a cure could run $100 or more.*

hydraulic valve lifters cause engine tapping sounds when they misbehave, and the result is engine misfire. You may hear these tapping sounds when you first start the engine, but they go away in a minute or so in a properly running engine, just as soon as the engine pumps up a supply of oil to get them filled. When the tapping noise doesn't go away, there is a chance that the lifters are defective. There is also the possibility that the noise is caused by wear in the valve train and, on Fords and Chevrolets, there is a simple adjustment to compensate and eliminate the problem. If you have one of these cars, you should ask about an adjustment before considering the possibility of replacing the lifters, as replacement can cost over $100 on a V-8 car.

To preclude lifter problems, have your engine oil and oil filter changed every 4000 miles or three months, whichever comes first. A clean lubricant is your best defense against this problem and premature engine wear as well.

COOLING SYSTEM

An engine develops a lot of heat, the temperatures in the combustion chamber reaching several thousand degrees. The cooling system carries away the heat, using one of two methods.

Water cooling is the most popular method. The engine head and block have passages through which water (and anti-freeze) is pumped, *See Fig. 22 A and B*. The water absorbs heat from the engine and carries it through a rubber hose into the radiator, a finned rectangle of tubes exposed to the air. The water cools as it passes through the radiator and then travels through another rubber hose back into the engine again. The water is kept moving in the circuit by a small pump bolted to the engine and is pulley-driven by a belt from the crankshaft pulley.

When the engine is cold, a thermostat blocks the flow of water to the radiator, so the hot water remains in the en-

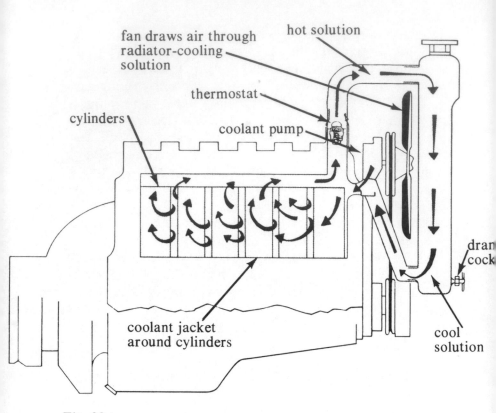

fan draws air through radiator-cooling solution

hot solution

thermostat

cylinders

coolant pump

drain cock

coolant jacket around cylinders

cool solution

Fig. 22A

Fig. 22. A   *This schematic drawing should give you a basic idea of how the cooling system works. The radiator in front gets rid of the heated water that the water pump mounted on the engine pumps into it. The water pump is on the exterior of the engine (driven by a belt from the crankshaft), but it projects into the water passages through a hole in the engine block, so it can circulate the water. Hoses connect the radiator to the engine, and a fan mounted on the water pump pulley draws air through the radiator. The cut-apart view of a section of a V-8 engine block (Fig. 22 B) should illustrate the system of cooling water passages in the engine.*

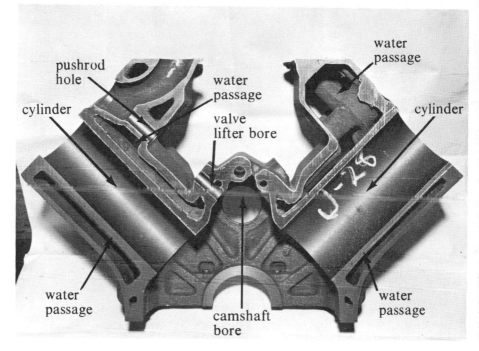

water passage

pushrod hole

cylinder

water passage

valve lifter bore

water passage

cylinder

water passage

water passage

camshaft bore

Fig. 22B

gine. When the engine reaches its operating temperature (the temperature it has been designed to operate most efficiently at), the thermostat opens, allowing water to be pumped to the radiator.

The cooling system is designed to operate under pressure, as this raises the boiling point of the water (nearly three degrees for every pound of pressure), and the radiator has a cap that holds 12 to 15 pounds of pressure. Anti-freeze in the water not only keeps the water from freezing in winter, but also raises its boiling point in summer. The combination of a pressure cap and 50% anti-freeze raises the boiling point to more than 265 degrees F. When unusual operating conditions (like excessive stop-and-go driving in bumper-to-bumper traffic) raise the temperature of the water-anti-freeze solution to much higher levels, the pressure exceeds design specifications, and a valve in the radiator cap opens to allow some water to escape. This explains the mini puddle you sometimes see at the front of the car after you stop driving in hot weather. Periodically top up the radiator with a 50-50 mixture of water and anti-freeze.

Air flow through the radiator is minimal at low car speed, so a fan is used to help draw air through. The fan is normally bolted to the water pump pulley, so as the belt spins the pump pulley, it also spins the fan. Many cars, particularly those with air conditioning, have a thermostatic control built into the fan assembly, so that the fan is disengaged when the engine is at operating temperature or below.

Air cooling is used on a few cars, the most popular being the Volkswagen. In this design, a belt-driven fan is enclosed in a sheet metal housing with a set of flaps controlled by a thermostat. When the air next to the engine reaches a certain temperature, the thermostat opens, pulling a rod that repositions the flaps so that air flow from the fan blows over the engine to cool it.

What Goes Wrong

An engine can operate at too low a temperature in winter just as easily as it can run at too high a temperature in summer.

The usual cause of too low a temperature is a defective engine thermostat. The results are poor engine operation (the engine doesn't reach the ideal operating temperature) and inadequate output from the heater (which is supplied by hot water from the engine).

Overheating is a more obvious problem, and it has many possible causes. Among them are:

1. A radiator cap that doesn't hold the specified pressure, which lowers the boiling point of the water-anti-freeze solution.

2. An inadequate amount of anti-freeze in the coolant. A 50% solution (half water, half anti-freeze) is the minimum acceptable, and 70% anti-freeze is even better.

3. A radiator clogged with rust scales.

4. Water leaks from a defective hose, water pump or radiator.

5. A defective water pump.

6. A loose drive belt.

7. A defective thermostat.

FUEL AND EXHAUST SYSTEMS

An engine burns 14 parts of air (by volume) for every part of gasoline, so the fuel system not only must deliver the fuel, but must mix it in proper proportions with air.

Virtually all cars have a mechanical fuel delivery system with a carburetor. Gasoline is delivered by a little device called a fuel pump, which is bolted to the engine on most cars (a few have electric units at or in the gas tank). The pump is connected by one tube to the gas tank, and by another to the carburetor, the unit that mixes the fuel with air and sprays it into the engine, *See Fig. 23.*

The fuel pump is much like a hand-operated bicycle air pump, in which a handle draws in air on the upstroke and pushes it into the tire on the downstroke. In the automobile fuel pump, a heavy spring is attached to the handle, and the handle is pushed by a cam on the camshaft. When the cam pushes the handle (up or down, depending on how the pump is designed), the pump draws in fuel from the tank. As the camshaft rotates, the cam releases pressure on the handle and the spring pushes it the other way, pumping fuel up to the carburetor.

As the fuel flows up to the carburetor, it passes through a filter, which may be in the tubing or at the point where the fuel enters the carburetor.

The carburetor operates like a combination perfume

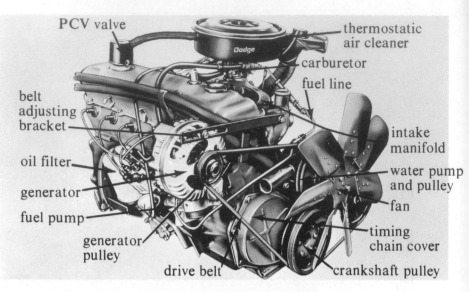

PCV valve

thermostatic air cleaner

carburetor

fuel line

belt adjusting bracket

intake manifold

oil filter

generator

fuel pump

water pump and pulley

fan

generator pulley

timing chain cover

drive belt

crankshaft pulley

Fig. 23. *Some of these parts, such as the PCV valve and thermostatic air cleaner, haven't been covered yet, but the picture gives a good idea of the layout of parts that have been discussed, such as the bracket with the elongated hole for adjusting tension of a belt. Notice the reference to the fuel pump—half-hidden by the AC generator (alternator)—which we also haven't covered yet. For now, just be aware of this unit mounted on the side of the engine, with a tube called the fuel line that goes up to the carburetor (the part with the air cleaner on it) and connected by another line to the gas tank (which you can't see in this picture). It can thus draw fuel from the tank and pump it up to the carburetor.*

atomizer and flush toilet (the perfume companies may dislike the comparison, but you'll see what we mean). In an atomizer, you squeeze the rubber bulb and a spray comes out a tiny hole. What you are doing is pushing air past the tube to the perfume, which draws the perfume out, mixes with it and forces the mixture out the little hole.

In a carburetor, the equivalent of the rubber air bulb is a specially shaped cylinder called an air horn, which has a round plate (called the throttle) across it. This throttle plate is mounted on a thin shaft and is connected by linkage to the gas pedal, *See Fig. 24*.

The downstroke of the pistons creates a vacuum in the cylinders, so when you step on the gas pedal and the throttle plate pivots open, air rushes into the engine to fill the vacuum through the carburetor air horn. A narrow tube from the fuel storage bowl in the carburetor projects into the air horn, and the air rushing by draws fuel out of the tube and mixes with it to create a combustible mixture, *See Fig. 25A*.

As you push the gas pedal down, you pivot the throttle plate further toward the position that allows the maximum amount of air flow through the air horn. The greater the air flow, the more fuel that is drawn out of the bowl, and the greater the amount of combustible air-fuel mixture that gets into the engine. The greater the number of air fuel charges that can get into the engine, the faster it runs and the more power it develops.

The method of storing fuel in the carburetor is like a flush toilet arrangement. If you lift the cover of the toilet tank and flush, you will see that a float drops to the bottom as the water leaves, and rises as a fresh supply of water pours in. At a certain point, an arm to which the float is attached closes a valve to shut off the water supply.

In a carburetor, there is also a tank (called the fuel bowl) with a float and an arm, plus a valve. When the fuel in the bowl rises to a certain level, the float also rises and a tab on its arm pushes a tapered needle into a seat, closing off the fuel supply from the pump. As fuel is consumed, the float drops, fuel under pressure pushes the needle off the seat and fuel flows into the bowl.

The air-fuel mixture that rushes through the carburetor air horn is distributed to each cylinder by an intake manifold, *See Fig. 25B*. This is a metal structure with chambers that lead from the carburetor base to the side of the cy-

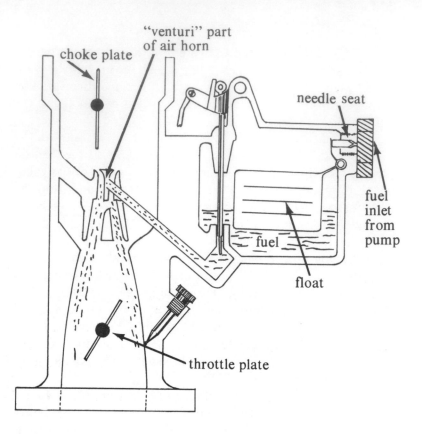

Fig. 24. *Fuel comes into the carburetor through a tubing connection at the right (labeled "fuel inlet from pump"). It flows into a bowl with a float which, when there's enough fuel in the bowl, rises and pushes a needle into a seat, closing off the fuel supply. When you step on the gas pedal, you pivot the throttle plate toward the vertical position, which allows air to rush into the section called the air horn and draw fuel from the bowl in a section of the air horn called the "venturi." The action is the same as that in a perfume atomizer: the result is that a fine spray of air and fuel enters the intake manifold, a pipelike part that carries the mixture to the intake port of the cylinder head. As the intake valve opens, the mixture flows into the cylinder. The choke plate at the top of the carburetor is shown in the vertical position (fully open). When the engine is cold, the choke blocks off the air horn, making the air-fuel mixture very rich with fuel. Inasmuch as an engine needs a rich fuel mixture for starting in cold weather, the choke is an indispensable aid.*

HOW MANY BARRELS

The simple carburetor outlined in this chapter is similar to what is found on most four- and six-cylinder engines. The popular V-8, however, has a carburetor with more than one air horn, typically two or four. The more air horns (also called barrels), the more air-fuel mixture that is admitted to feed the engine. Hence the greater power the engine develops.

In identifying carburetors, the terms one-barrel, two-barrel and four-barrel are commonly used. You must be able to identify your carburetor if you plan to do any maintenance yourself, because many catalog parts listings are based on this information.

Lift off the air cleaner cover as described on page 143, "Replacing an Air Filter," look into the top of the carburetor and count the number of circular openings. The illustration below gives an example.

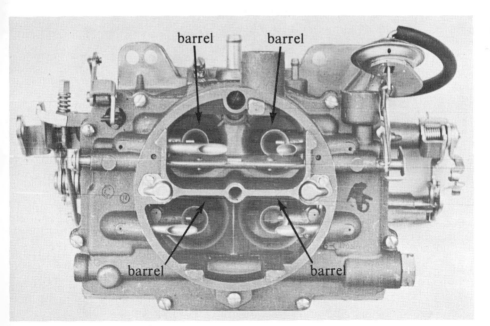

barrel   barrel

barrel   barrel

Fig. 24A

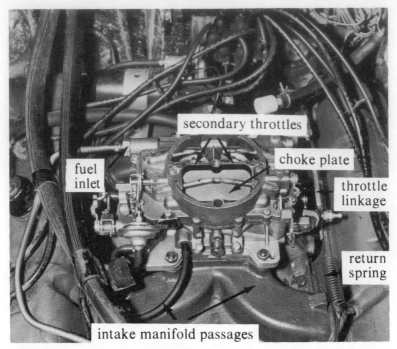

Fig. 25A

Fig. 25. A *In this view of a four-barrel carburetor on its intake manifold, the four barrels (air horns) are not all visible.*
Two, called the primaries, are covered by the choke plate, which is closed. The secondaries, which only open at high engine speed, are very visible, as are the exteriors of two of the intake manifold's passages to the cylinder head ports of this V-8. The throttle linkage is the connection between the carburetor's throttle plate and the gas pedal, and the return spring is what returns the gas pedal to the normal position when you remove your foot. In Fig. 25B, which shows an intake manifold all by itself, you see two holes in the center (for a two-barrel carburetor) and four passages (each one to two intake ports in a V-8 engine). The five-sided hole is for the thermostatic control for the automatic choke while the round hole at the right is just an opening to the camshaft of the distributor, which in this engine just happens to be mounted on the intake manifold.

linder head, where there are "ports" (passages) that lead to the combustion chambers. At the right instant, the intake valve of a combustion chamber opens and the air-fuel mix-

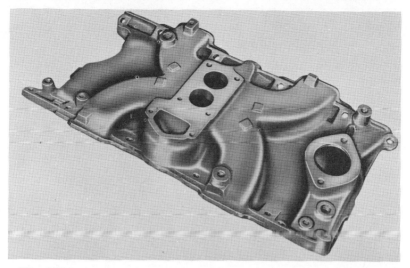

Fig. 25B

ture flows into the combustion chamber. The valve then closes, the mixture is compressed and ignited, and after the piston has been pushed down to develop power, the exhaust valve opens. The crankshaft then moves the piston up to push the burned gases out of the cylinder.

The exhaust gases go out through separate ports (called exhaust ports) and into another chambered component (called the exhaust manifold), *See Fig. 26 A and B.* The exhaust manifold channels the exhaust gases into piping that takes them to the muffler, which dampens the noise of the gas flow.

There are several important accessories in the fuel system with which you should be familiar: the choke, the heat riser and the air cleaner.

The automatic choke is the most widely used type today. It's a circular plate that looks like a throttle, but it's near the top of the carburetor air horn and is connected to a thermostatic system, *See Figs. 24 and 25.* When the engine is cold, it blocks the air horn, restricting the air flow through the carburetor. As the engine warms up, the plate pivots to

51

PCV valve

in-line gasoline
filter

exhaust
manifold

Fig. 26A

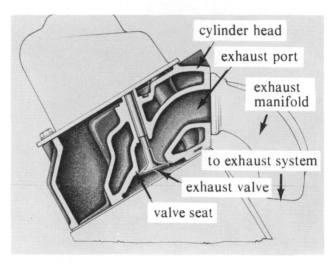

cylinder head

exhaust port

exhaust
manifold

to exhaust system

exhaust valve

valve seat

Fig. 26B   *This engine clearly shows the in-line gasoline filter (used primarily on cars made by Chrysler Corporation), the exhaust manifold (without the rest of the exhaust system) and the PCV valve (see the section on Pollution Control Devices later in this chapter). Fig. 26B should clear some things up for you: the exhaust valve is closed, but when it is pushed down off its seat, exhaust gases can enter the exhaust port and flow straight into the exhaust manifold, which is bolted onto the side of the engine, covering the exhaust ports.*

allow more and more air flow. The reason for the choke is to provide a richer fuel mixture (more fuel in the mixture), which the engine needs for starting in cold weather.

Some European cars have a manual choke, operated by a cable to a knob on the dashboard.

The air cleaner filters the air that enters the carburetor air horn, removing abrasive dirt particles that could harm the engine. It sits in a big sheet metal housing on top of the engine.

The heat riser, also called a manifold heat control valve, is built into the exhaust manifold, *See Fig. 27*. It works somewhat like an automatic choke, incorporating a pivoting plate and a thermostatic control. When the engine is cold, it allows hot exhaust gases to move into a chamber in the exhaust manifold that bears against the intake manifold. The exhaust heats the intake manifold, which helps vaporize the air-fuel mixture to make it even more combustible. When the engine is warm enough to do this job, the valve pivots into a closed position, keeping exhaust gas away from the intake manifold.

What Goes Wrong

The fuel system has two filters, and both should be changed periodically. One is the gasoline filter, which when clogged can block the flow of fuel, *See Fig. 26 A*. The other is the air filter, which when filled with dirt can restrict the flow of air, resulting in an air-fuel mixture that has too high a percentage of fuel (it may be combustible, but gas mileage is reduced). The air filter is particularly easy to replace (see page 143).

The fuel pump normally lasts at least 50,000 miles. When it fails, it usually doesn't provide enough fuel to keep the engine running under all conditions. Most fuel pumps can be tested and replaced when necessary in less than half an hour.

The carburetor is a sensitive device with many little valves and pumplike systems to provide extra fuel when

Fig. 27. *An exhaust manifold with a heat riser at the bottom. The close-up look below shows the heat riser itself. The external parts control a pivoting plate assembly inside to preheat the intake manifold in cold weather.*

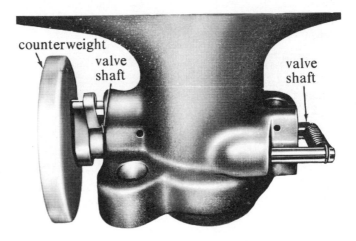

counterweight

valve shaft

valve shaft

needed for acceleration. Most of these devices perform acceptably for the life of the car. The smog controls used on today's cars impose limits on how smooth engine performance can be, and motorists too often blame the carburetor for rough engine idling and less-than-flashing acceleration.

The most common carburetor problems are caused by dirt. So if your car has a gas filter and you replace it periodically, you should have few problems here.

Even with a clean carburetor, however, you may experience flooding, which means that an excessive amount of fuel is getting into the bowl and then into the engine. When there's much too much gasoline in the air-fuel mixture, it won't burn and the engine stalls. There are three possible causes:

1. Failure of the needle and seat valve assembly to close off the fuel flow into the bowl.
2. A float arm that is out of adjustment, allowing the fuel level to rise too high.
3. Excessive fuel pump pressure which pushes open the needle valve (this one is rare).

You can tell when a carburetor is stalling because of flooding by the technique needed to restart. If you must hold the gas pedal to the floor, the problem is flooding. If this seems contradictory, the reason is this: when you floor the gas pedal, you permit the maximum amount of air to mix with the excessive amount of fuel, and the overall result is a mixture that, while still overly rich with fuel, can be burned. Note: on a hot day, many cars will show some signs of flooding when they stall, but you've only got a flooding problem if it occurs at normal temperatures (both engine and air temperatures), and the choke is working properly.

The automatic choke is subject to trouble. The thermostatic device that controls it may lose effectiveness and the vacuum device that pulls it may stick. In either case, the choke may remain closed when the engine is warm, resulting in a mixture that is borderline rich with fuel. This may also cause stalling, and restarting may require flooring the gas pedal.

The heat riser is definitely prone to sticking—closed or open. It should be sprayed with penetrating oil as part of an engine tuneup. Ask the mechanic to do this, for most won't without a request. A heat riser that sticks in the heat-off position will cause engine stumble on warmup. One that sticks in the heat-on position will cause overheating of the fuel-air mixture, evaporating much of it, and the engine will stall.

The exhaust system has no moving parts aside from the heat riser, but it is subject to rustout and damage from road debris. Holes in the exhaust piping or muffler produce loud noises.

ENGINE MOUNTS

You may have heard of the engine mounts, for not too long ago they were the subjects of manufacturers' recalls. The engine mounts are the brackets that hold the engine to the body. The mount is a sandwich with metal slices of bread and a rubber filling that absorbs engine shake without transmitting most of it to the car body, *See Fig. 28.*

What Goes Wrong

As the rubber deteriorates from exposure to air, grease, oil and road film, it loses its ability to absorb shake and still hold reasonably firm. It soon permits the engine to move from side to side and forward.

This movement can pull on the linkage to the gas pedal, and when you suddenly take your foot off the pedal, the throttle can snap closed. This sudden closing can stall the engine. Or the mount may permit so much forward movement that the fan, perhaps a couple of inches or less from the radiator in a new car, may be pushed into it, destroying both parts.

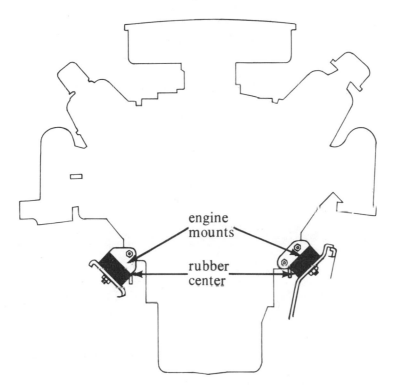

Fig. 28. *The engine mounts are rubber sandwiches (slabs of metal with rubber in between) that bolt the engine to the body. The rubber absorbs most engine shake without transmitting it to the body. Deterioration of the rubber can let the engine move excessively, and under extreme conditions this movement can cause the engine to stall or even allow the fan to go into the radiator, damaging both parts.*

Late-model cars all have safety mounts—if the rubber fails in these, the mount will lock metal parts together. This will result in terrible vibration, forcing you to take the car in for replacement of the mounts, but should prevent the sudden engine stalls or damage to the fan and radiator.

IGNITION SYSTEM

The ignition system turns battery current into high-voltage electricity that creates a spark at the spark plugs—little terminals that thread into the combustion chambers. When they "spark," they set fire to the air-fuel mixture.

Let's look at the components.

Coil: Here's where the high voltage for the plugs is created. The coil is an electromagnet—an iron core around which comparatively thick wire is wound, *See Fig. 29.* When

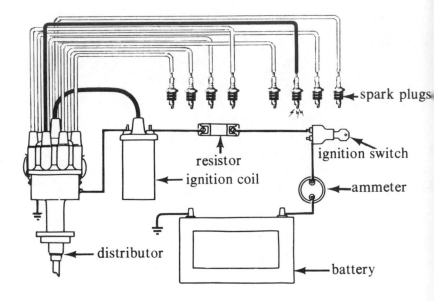

Fig. 29. *The basic ignition circuit. When you turn the ignition switch to "on," you complete a circuit from the battery through the ammeter, through the ignition switch, through a resistor, through the ignition coil, and into the distributor to the breaker points. When the breaker points open, high voltage is developed in the coil, which transmits it through the center wire into the top of the distributor, where it is sent by the rotor to the appropriate spark plug wire, which carries it to the plug, which explodes the air-fuel mixture in the combustion chamber.*

battery current passes through the coil, it creates a magnetic field (an area of magnetic attraction) around it. There is a second winding of finer wire around the first, and it is a principle of electricity that if a current is transferred from a few windings of thick wire to many windings of thin wire, the voltage (electrical pressure) is increased. This principle is used by public utilities in their high-voltage transformers, and an ignition coil is really a transformer.

Distributor, *See Figs. 30 A, B and C:* here's where all the mechanical action takes place, so look at it closely. It has a plastic cover that holds thick wires that go to the spark plugs (one to each plug). Remove the plastic cover, called a distributor cap, and you can see a shaft in the center of the distributor body. This shaft has a small gear at the bottom that meshes with a gear on the camshaft. As the camshaft spins, so does this shaft.

The spinning of the distributor shaft does triple duty, but we will consider one job at a time. First, notice the piece of plastic on top of the shaft, the one with the metal pointer. It's called the rotor and as it spins, it aligns with little pieces of metal embedded in the distributor cap. These pieces of metal are connected to the spark plug wires. Clearly, if we can get the spark to the rotor, we can pass it to the appropriate spark plug wire, which will carry it to the spark plug. This is done by a thick wire (that looks like a spark plug wire) from the center of the coil to the center of the distributor cap. Notice the projecting piece of metal from the rotor: when the cap is on, it is in light contact with the metal insert in the cap that holds the wire from the center of the coil.

So there's the picture. The engine camshaft spins the distributor shaft, which momentarily aligns the rotor with metal tabs that connect to the spark plug wires. By proper engine and ignition system design, the rotor will always transfer the electricity from the coil to the right spark plug wire.

Now let's consider the creation of the spark itself. The first thing you should know is that it isn't really a spark, but

Fig. 30. A *Here the distributor is completely apart. The cap is shown with the spark plug wires removed, but as you know, they fit into those towers. When the distributor is assembled, the rotor sits on top of the distributor shaft and spins with the camshaft. It picks up the spark from the coil (through the wire into the center of the distributor cap) and distributes it to each plug wire tower by means of little electrical contacts inside (labeled "A" in Fig. 30B).*

Now turn to the ignition breaker points (Fig. 30C). In the assembled distributor, they are screwed onto the contact plate (also called the breaker plate) and bear against the distributor cam. One of the two points is fixed in place, the other is on a pivot. As the cam turns, it is in constant touch with a little fiber block called the cam follower or rubbing block. As you can see, the points are closed when the follower is in contact with a flat part of the cam, and they pop open when it comes in contact with a high spot. In the typical distributor, there is one high spot on the cam for every cylinder, and every time the points open, a spark goes to a spark plug. The system is designed so that the right plug gets the spark every time.

Now notice the centrifugal advance weights, which are mounted on springs. At high speeds they swing outward and move the upper part of the distributor shaft to alter the time that the points open, which changes the timing of the spark to meet different engine conditions. A similar function is performed by the vacuum chamber, which responds to changes in engine vacuum and moves the contact plate on which the points are mounted, pivoting it back and forth and thus changing the time the breaker points open—all according to car operating conditions which are reflected by changes in vacuum developed in the engine.

60

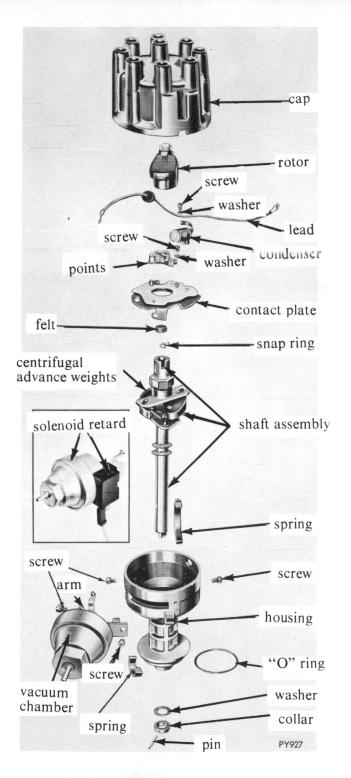

cap

rotor

screw

washer

lead

screw

condenser

washer

points

contact plate

felt

snap ring

centrifugal
advance weights

solenoid retard

shaft assembly

spring

screw

arm

screw

housing

vacuum
chamber

"O" ring

screw

washer

spring

collar

pin

61

PY927

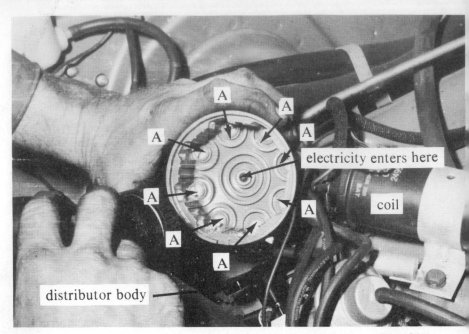

A

A

A

A

electricity enters here

A

coil

A

A

A

distributor body

Fig. 30B

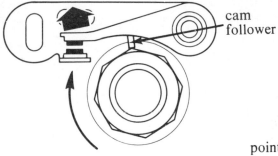

cam
follower

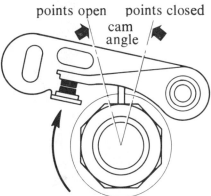

points open   points closed
cam
angle

Fig. 30C

a surge of that high-voltage electricity across two electrodes (metal prongs that conduct electricity). As you can see in *Fig. 31,* the spark plug has a center electrode, down which

Fig. 31. *This is the glamour part of the ignition system—the spark plug. It has no moving parts, and the spark is really just high-voltage electricity created elsewhere, jumping a gap between two electrical conductors called electrodes. The plug illustrated has a resistor built into it, which reduces ignition system interference with the car radio.*

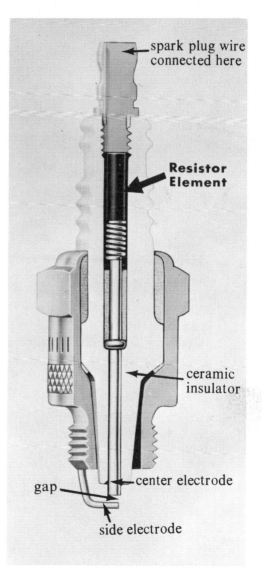

spark plug wire connected here

Resistor Element

ceramic insulator

center electrode

gap

side electrode

the current from the plug wire flows. When the electricity gets to the end of the electrode, it is trying to keep going.

Electricity takes the path of least resistance, and in a normal spark plug, it is a short jump to the other electrode. This jump through a gap is the "spark" that ignites the air-fuel mixture. When the current reaches the second electrode, its trip is over, for this second electrode is in metallic contact (electrically conductive) with the engine, as is the car battery (via a cable) and the circuit is complete.

It takes a lot of electrical pressure—voltage—for a spark to jump the gap—perhaps as much as 20,000 volts, although usually a lot less. The 12-volt battery in the car can supply only 12 volts. Thus we must increase 12 volts to as much as 20,000 volts. Here is where the coil's second winding becomes important. You will remember we just discussed how to increase voltage by transferring battery current from the first winding to the second one.

The layout of the windings of wire in the ignition coil is such that if the circuit through the first winding is suddenly opened, the electromagnetic field will collapse, right into the second, finer windings.

To suddenly open the battery current circuit, we go back to the distributor shaft. We said it did triple duty, and now we'll look at its second job: flipping a switch to open the circuit through the first coil winding.

A wire is run from the relatively thicker coil wire windings into the distributor body, and to one of a pair of metal contacts called ignition breaker points. When the two metal contacts touch, just as in an ordinary switch, the circuit from the battery through the coil is complete and an electromagnetic field builds up in the coil. When one of the contacts is pushed away, the circuit opens and the magnetic field collapses on the fine windings in the coil, producing high voltage, *See Figs. 29 and 30.*

The pushing away of the contact is done on a regular schedule by a specially shaped portion of the distributor shaft (called the distributor cam). If you'll recall our discussion of the engine camshaft, a cam was described as a teardrop-shaped protrusion. In the distributor, the cam is some-what different—there are evenly spaced high spots, one for each cylinder. As the distributor shaft is rotated by the engine camshaft, the high spots push the breaker points open, then allow a spring to close them, then push them open, then allow them to close, etc. Because electricity travels at a speed of 186,000 miles per second (the speed of light), the pushing open of the points instantaneously produces a spark at a plug. When the points close, the magnetic field builds up in the coil. When they open, it collapses to produce the high voltage for the plugs. Note: some distributors have two sets of breaker points, so each high spot on the cam can open the coil circuit twice. In this design, only four high spots are needed for an eight-cylinder engine.

If you look at the coil and distributor, you may wonder why the wire from the center of the coil to the center of the distributor cap is much thicker than the coil's other two wires, especially since the center wire supposedly comes from finer windings and the thinner wires are part of the 12-volt thick-wire circuit that creates the magnetic field. The answer is that the thick wire is really thin—it just has a very heavy layer of rubber or plastic insulation to help hold in the high voltage.

There are three other parts of the ignition system that perform important jobs: the condenser, the resistor, and the spark timing and advance system.

The condenser is an electrical shock absorber. When the field in the coil collapses, some of the current tries to flow through the thick-wire circuit to the breaker points. If this were allowed to happen, the current would burn the points, and the lost current would weaken the high-voltage spark to the level where it might not be able to jump the gap in the spark plug. The condenser provides a temporary storage for this current, which it later discharges back into the coil.

The resistor is an electrical barrier that reduces the voltage from battery to coil from 12 to about 8 or 9. Why reduce the battery voltage through the coil? Won't that reduce the voltage increase when the magnetic field collapses in the coil? The answer is yes, but there are other considerations:

1. Lower voltage means less current to the breaker points, so they don't burn out until many thousands of miles.
2. The reduced current keeps the coil operating at a safe temperature.
3. Even at the lower voltage, the coil output is normally quite adequate.

The only time that the engine really needs the maximum possible voltage for the spark plugs is during the hard job—starting. At this time only, the resistor is bypassed and there is full voltage through the coil and breaker points.

The timing and advance system is perhaps the most sophisticated part of the ignition system. It has the job of varying the arrival of the spark at the plug according to engine operating conditions. The basic timing of the spark (called spark timing or ignition timing) is specified by the car manufacturer and is checked with a special tool called a timing light which is aimed at reference marks on the engine and crankshaft pulley. If the basic timing is correct, the marks will be aligned when the light is turned on. Incorrect timing is adjusted by minor shifts in the position of the distributor body, which is bolted to the engine.

Once the basic timing is correctly set, the ignition system's automatic controls take over. One is the vacuum advance, which measures the amount of engine vacuum in the intake manifold (the vacuum varies according to foot pressure on the gas pedal). The other is the centrifugal advance, which gets us to the third job of the distributor shaft.

On some cars, you can see the centrifugal advance when the distributor cap is removed, *See Fig. 32*. On most other cars, however, it is located under the plate that holds the breaker points, and so is out of sight.

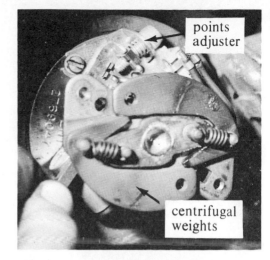

Fig. 32. *This is a General Motors V-8 engine distributor with the cap, rotor and radio interference shield off, giving you a close-up look at the centrifugal weights and their spring mounting, which is on top of the distributor shaft and not, as in other designs, hidden under the breaker plate.*

points adjuster

centrifugal weights

The centrifugal advance consists of spring-loaded half-moon-shaped weights connected to the distributor shaft, which is really a two-piece assembly. When engine speed is high, centrifugal force (remember that from high school science?) moves the weights away from the shaft, turning the distributor cam backward, so that the ignition points are pushed open a bit earlier than otherwise.

Tailoring the arrival of the spark according to engine vacuum and speed used to be done primarily to improve performance and gas mileage. Today, the vacuum advance systems are sometimes used in reverse—to delay the arrival of the sparks for lower exhaust emissions. Some cars have vacuum systems that both advance and retard the spark, according to performance and emission requirements.

ELECTRONIC IGNITION SYSTEMS

Many late-model cars are being equipped with electronic ignition systems, which eliminate the breaker points and condenser. There is still a distributor, but instead of a distributor cam on the shaft, there is a toothed unit. When a tooth aligns with an electronic device (called a pickup), it creates an impulse to a transistor circuit, that opens the battery current circuit through the coil.

What Goes Wrong

There are so many things that can go wrong with a conventional ignition system, it would be impossible to list them all. The most common are:

1. Wearing out of the spark plugs.
2. Wearing out or burning of the ignition breaker points.
3. Failure of the coil or condenser.
4. Poor or broken electrical connections.
5. Cracking of the distributor cap or rotor.
6. Failure of the resistor.
7. Cracking or oil soaking of the spark plug wires.
8. Excessive wear of the distributor cam high spots.
9. Excessive wear of the distributor shaft bearing (a smooth cylindrical sleeve that supports the shaft).
10. Buildup of electrical corrosion in the distributor cap retainers for the plug wires.

The first six problems will usually prevent the engine from running altogether. The latter four are more likely to cause only hard starting and poor engine operation.

Although the vacuum and centrifugal advance mechanisms are basically reliable, their minor malfunctioning may impede engine performance.

The electronic ignition system is subject to all the problems of the conventional system except for problems with the distributor cam, breaker points and condenser, which they don't have. However, the electronic components themselves are subject to failure. Nevertheless, the overall reliability of electronic ignition systems is expected to be good.

STARTING SYSTEM

When you turn the key to the start position, you are completing a circuit from the battery to a special kind of switch (called a starter solenoid) usually mounted on top of the starting motor. *See Fig. 33 A.* When this switch closes, it completes a second circuit from the battery to the starter, which is a DC electric motor.

The separate circuits are used because the starter draws a great deal of current, and it is impractical to make the key switch substantial enough to carry this current. The key switch only carries the small amount of current necessary to close the solenoid.

When the starter is energized with current, it moves a small gear, *See Fig. 33 B,* into mesh with a large gear

Fig. 33. A *In Fig. 14, you saw how the starter is mounted against the rear of the engine. Here's a look at what happens. At the starter, the turning of the key to the start position energizes the solenoid, which pushes the pinion gear forward and into mesh with a large gear pressed onto the rim of the flywheel. The little pinion turns very fast, but the flywheel turns slowly. However, there is enough energy transferred to the flywheel (and the crankshaft to which it is bolted) so that the pistons move up and down, the valves open and close, the fuel pump pumps and the ignition system fires—and quickly the engine is running on its own. Fig. 33B shows the relationship of the two gears: the big gear on the rim of the flywheel is at the right, the little gear from the starter is on the left.*

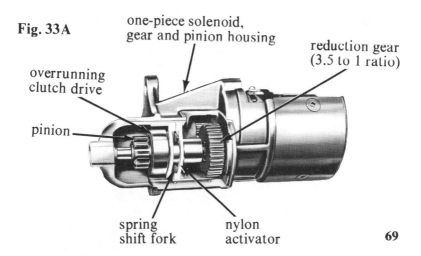

Fig. 33A

one-piece solenoid, gear and pinion housing

reduction gear (3.5 to 1 ratio)

overrunning clutch drive

pinion

spring shift fork

nylon activator

69

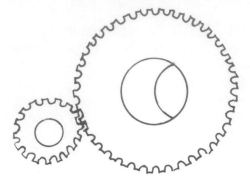

around the circumference of the engine flywheel. The starter also turns the gear, turning the flywheel, and because the flywheel is bolted to the crankshaft, the crankshaft turns, moving the pistons up and down and spinning the camshaft. The camshaft operates the fuel and ignition systems and the engine is soon running on its own.

What Goes Wrong

A weak battery and loose or electrically corroded battery cables are the prime causes of starting troubles, *See Fig. 34.*

If the battery and cables are in good condition and tight, and you don't hear a click when you turn the key to start position, there is reason to suspect that the solenoid is

Fig. 34. *What seems to be a dead battery may actually be a poor connection caused by corrosion deposits on the cables. Wire brush them off and the battery may be as good as new.*

defective, for it is the solenoid that makes the distinctive clicking sound as it closes, immediately prior to the familiar sound of the engine cranking.

The starter itself may also fail, but it is basically a reliable component. The only trouble it normally encounters is failure of its little gear, called the starter drive, to engage the flywheel gear. In this case, you may hear the click and the whirring sound of the starter, but not the sound of the engine turning.

Sluggish engine cranking normally is caused by a weak battery or poor cable connections, but in winter may also be caused by excessively thick oil, such as that used in summer, or by over use of an oil thickening additive, which has the same effect.

CHARGING SYSTEM

The charging system has the job of keeping the battery charged and supplying current for the operation of the ignition system and other electrical components. Its primary components are a generator, which produces the electricity, and a voltage regulator, which controls generator output according to the needs of the battery and the electrical units in the car.

The generator, *See Fig. 23,* works like an electric motor—but in reverse. The motor takes electricity (from the battery, for example) and converts it into mechanical energy (the motor spins). The generator is driven mechanically (by a belt from the crankshaft pulley) and its internal design converts the mechanical energy into electricity.

The physical principles behind the operation of a motor or generator involve the laws of magnetism and the details are rather complex. It should be some comfort to know that most mechanics have no idea how these units work either. They just know how to test them and when they find them defective, unbolt them and install replacements.

Most cars today have AC generators (called alternators). They produce alternating current (like that in your home), which is converted to direct current (necessary for a car) by electronic components called diodes. Older cars and a few imported cars have DC generators. The alternator is the favorite, for although it costs a bit more, it weighs less and produces much more current at low engine speeds.

The voltage regulator controls generator output in one of two ways: with a transistor circuit that includes voltage-sensitive electronic components, or with a mechanical circuit of breaker points (somewhat similar to ignition breaker points) and voltage-sensing electromagnets.

Some transistorized regulators are so small they are built into the alternators.

What Goes Wrong

If the dashboard gauge or warning light shows that the generator is discharging, you should have at least half an hour to find help, for the car will operate on battery current. With a fully charged battery in warm weather, you may be able to go for up to two hours or more if you turn off most of the car's electrical accessories.

A sudden indication of discharge probably means a drive belt has snapped or that a wire has come off or broken.

A battery that is constantly weak may indicate inadequate output of current from the charging system, which can be caused by a loose belt, or defects in the generator or regulator.

POLLUTION CONTROL DEVICES

The devices built into your car to reduce smog are generally fail-safe. That is, when they fail, they do not interfere with the basic operation of the car.

The two exceptions are the Positive Crankcase Ventilation (PCV) System and the Thermostatic Air Cleaner, so they're worth discussing.

POSITIVE CRANKCASE VENTILATION

This system (*See Figs. 23 and 26*) purges the engine of

any fuel vapors that slip past the piston rings. In older cars, these vapors were expelled into the atmosphere, contributing to air pollution. On all current cars, there is a hose from the valve cover to the carburetor base that routes these vapors back into the combustion chambers for burning. The vapors mix with the air-fuel mixture and are drawn into the combustion chambers, where they are burned.

The amount of vapor that the engine can accept without performing poorly varies according to the load imposed on it. Therefore, a flow control device (called a PCV valve) is used, usually installed on the engine valve cover.

What Goes Wrong

If the PCV valve sticks in the closed position or becomes clogged by foreign particles in the vapors, excessive vapor pressures will build up in the engine. Under extreme conditions, these pressures can force their way out by destroying weak portions of gaskets that would otherwise survive. Once the gaskets are ruined, oil leaks result, so don't take chances. Replace the PCV valve once a year. It is inexpensive and takes only a couple of minutes to change.

THERMOSTATIC AIR CLEANER

Many late-model cars have a thermostatic device on the air cleaner that controls the source of air into the filter. At low temperatures, it moves a throttle-like plate to close off the air cleaner's air opening, forcing the air cleaner to draw air from a separate duct that is bolted to the hot exhaust manifold, *See Fig. 35.* The warm air vaporizes the fuel better, for improved combustibility.

What Goes Wrong

Any thermostatic device has lots of potential for trouble, but thermostatic air cleaners have proved to be reasonably reliable. To check the unit, start a cold engine and feel inside the air intake opening. The valve should have closed off the opening. When the engine is warm, feel inside again,

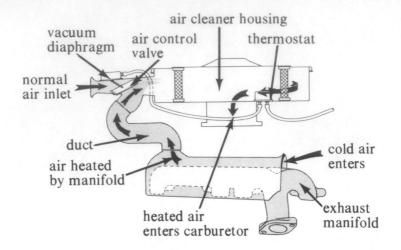

normal air inlet

vacuum diaphragm

air control valve

air cleaner housing

thermostat

duct

air heated by manifold

cold air enters

heated air enters carburetor

exhaust manifold

Fig. 35. *This drawing of the thermostatic air cleaner shows how a thermostatic device in the air cleaner housing controls a vacuum diaphragm to regulate the position of an air control valve. When the outside air is cold, the valve closes off the normal air inlet and instead air is drawn in from a duct over the exhaust manifold (hot) up into the air cleaner. As the air in the air cleaner is warmed by engine heat, the thermostat closes off this duct and outside air is channeled through the normal air inlet. Heating of the air when the engine is cold improves atomization of the air-fuel mixture for better combustion. This improves engine performance and reduces smog-causing exhaust emissions.*

and the valve should have moved downward, blocking off the duct to the exhaust manifold.

If the valve is not where it should be, the odds are that the thermostatic control must be replaced. A poor hose connection is also a possibility, so look around the air cleaner and see if any of the hoses are off at the air cleaner or wherever they should connect.

CLUTCH AND TORQUE CONVERTER

To permit the engine to run when the car is stopped, it must be possible to momentarily separate the engine from the rest of the drive train and let the transmission be shifted into a position that will not transfer power. This position is called Neutral.

In a manual transmission, the separation is done by the clutch. When you depress the clutch pedal, you are actuating a linkage setup in which a special type of bearing (called the clutch release, or throwout, bearing) pushes in the hub of a spring plate that holds a friction disc against the

Fig 36. *A manual clutch is not easy to visualize in operation. This drawing shows the parts: a flywheel (without the ring gear drawn in) is connected to the engine; clutch disc (coated with friction material) is mounted in grooves (called splines) on a shaft that goes into the transmission; pressure plate assembly (consisting of plate, spring and cover) is placed over the friction disc and is bolted to the flywheel. When you step on the clutch pedal, you move linkage connected to a device called a release, or throwout, bearing, which releases spring pressure on the clutch disc. The clutch disc then slides back on its splines from the flywheel. When you release the clutch pedal, the spring forces the clutch disc firmly against the flywheel, joining the engine (via the flywheel) to the transmission (via the shaft). You must break the connection (by stepping on the clutch pedal) every time you shift gears. You must reconnect (by releasing the clutch pedal) in order to join the engine connection (via the transmission) to the rear wheels and thus allow the car to move.*

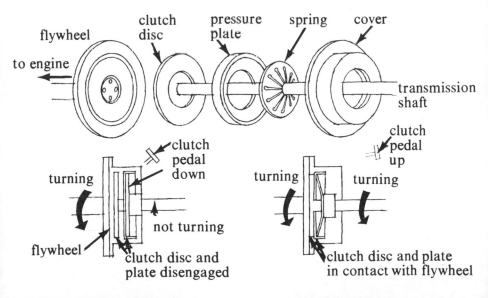

flywheel. Inasmuch as this disc is also mounted on a shaft from the transmission, it normally connects engine and transmission. Releasing the disc from its spring-loaded position against the flywheel temporarily severs the only connection between the two units, *See Fig. 36.*

Because it is the only connection, the clutch must hold firmly against the flywheel when the car is moving. When it doesn't, this is called clutch slippage. It results in lost power and requires replacement of the friction disc.

What Goes Wrong

The friction disc can fail, due to normal wear, driver abuse (resting the foot on the clutch pedal), or leakage of oil from the engine or transmission. The clutch release bearing can fail. Or the spring plate (called the pressure plate) can fail. In all these cases the defective part must be replaced.

TORQUE CONVERTER

The automatic transmission car doesn't use a clutch for the momentary separation, for the torque converter eliminates the need.

The torque converter is a sealed unit with two fanlike halves of a doughnut inside, in a chamber filled with transmission oil. One half is bolted to the engine, the other to the transmission. Visualize two fans very close together and mentally turn on one of them. The other will also start to spin, picking up motion through the air.

In the torque converter, motion is transmitted through the oil, and with proper design, there is very little motion lost. There is some, because the connection isn't really solid, but the clutch pedal is eliminated and that's a convenience.

We've left out one important part from the torque converter, so let's put it in now: the stator, *See Fig. 37.* This is a circular unit between the two doughnut halves. It has fins to direct oil flow most efficiently within the torque converter for maximum transfer of force without transfer of speed. Read that sentence over and before you say, "What are they

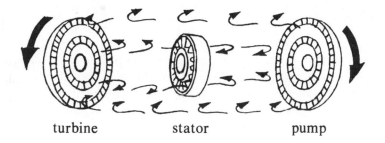

turbine   stator   pump

Fig. 37. *This is the inside of a torque converter. The "turbine" is the doughnut half bolted to the flywheel, the "pump" is the doughnut half bolted to a transmission shaft, while the stator in between is mounted on still another shaft. The arrows show that the stator directs oil flow for maximum transfer of energy without transfer of speed from turbine to pump; this is the equivalent of a big gear on the engine driving a little gear on the transmission.*

talking about?" we'll tell you that it's exactly what is done with gears of different sizes and the section on transmissions will (hopefully) clarify the principle.

To do its job, the stator must remain motionless as the car is accelerated from a stop, and then gradually spin so that it has no effect when the car is just cruising. This is accomplished by mounting the stator on a shaft with little devices that hold it from being turned counterclockwise (backward) by the force of the oil flow in the converter. As the car picks up speed and starts cruising, the two halves of the doughnut are soon moving at virtually the same speed. The oil performs almost like a solid mass in joining the two halves of the doughnut and this pulls the stator around in a clockwise direction, which releases the holding devices.

What Goes Wrong

The little holding devices of the stator may wear out, permitting the stator to be forced backward by oil pressure. This results in loss of normal acceleration below 30 or 35 mph.

TRANSMISSION

In order to move a car from a stopped position, we must be able to turn the engine fast, so it develops enough force to overcome the inertia of a body (the car) at rest. To be able to turn the engine fast, while the car itself moves slowly, and then gradually establish a close relationship between engine speed and increasing road speed, a transmission is used.

The transmission is a set of gears (remember the egg beater) that can be switched according to the road speed and the load being placed on the engine, *See Fig. 38.*

If we mesh a 12-tooth gear with a 36-tooth gear, and apply power to spin the 12-tooth, every complete revolution of the 12-tooth will only turn the 36-tooth gear one third of a revolution. If this larger gear is mounted on a shaft that leads to the rear wheels, you can see that the engine can run at a speed three times greater than that transmitted to the wheels.

Although the speed is reduced, the force is not, for the engine has not slowed down and the engine is the energy source. The principle of changing speed through gears, without losing energy, is used throughout the car. The small gear on the starter motor turns very fast, and the starter is using a lot of electrical energy. The big gear on the flywheel is turning very slowly. Although the flywheel is only spinning at a tiny fraction of the speed of the starter, the energy it absorbs is considerable.

The number of teeth on the gear is not really the determining factor—rather it is the relative circumferences of the two gears. In order for gear teeth to mesh, the teeth must be of the same size, so a 36-tooth gear must have a circumference three times that of a 12-tooth gear.

The principle also holds for pulleys. A pulley of 36-inch circumference will turn at one third the speed of one of 12-inch circumference if they are joined by a belt.

Now perhaps we can extend the principle of gear reduction without loss of energy to the torque converter, and

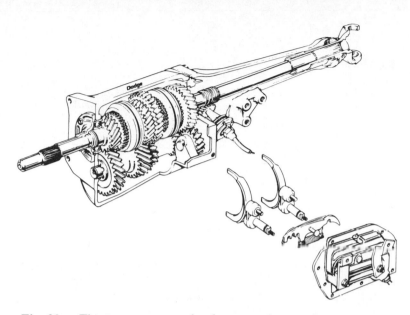

Fig. 38. *This is a cutaway of a three-speed manual transmission. All the gears are already in mesh, and shifting merely locks one on a shaft while permitting another to spin freely.*

clear up some of the mystery we left in the previous section.

By using the stator to direct oil flow, the engine half of the doughnut spins up to three times faster than the transmission doughnut, but the energy transferred is almost complete. The torque converter uses oil flow to create the same effect as meshing a large gear (the transmission doughnut) with a small one (the engine doughnut).

In the modern transmission itself, the changing of gear ratios is not done by sliding one gear into mesh with another (except for reverse gear). A transmission has all the gears already in mesh, but allows them to spin freely until needed. In a manual transmission, shifting gears is really moving a locking device along a shaft and against the gear, holding it. When the gear is turned, it turns the shaft too, sending power out through the rear of the transmission.

The automatic transmission is a complex combination of systems and a unit set of gears (called a planetary gear

Fig. 39. *This is a planetary gear set in an automatic transmission. This same gear arrangement was used in some olden-days bicycles and was also the gear set (in a manually operated version) in the old Model T Ford. Most mechanics still don't understand how it works.*

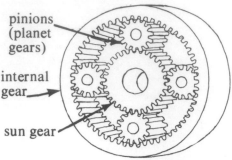

pinions (planet gears)

internal gear

sun gear

set) *(See Fig. 39)*. To explain its operation would require a separate book and a set of readers who are fascinated by mechanical minutiae.

What Goes Wrong

Manual transmission

1. Metallic grinding noise. This is caused by a low oil level or a worn bearing, the latter forcing an overhaul of the unit.
2. Difficulty in engaging gears. An adjustment of the linkage to the transmission usually cures this.
3. Grinding noise when engaging gears. The locking devices (called synchronizers) are probably worn, and the transmission will have to be overhauled.
4. Shift lever jumps out, putting car into neutral. The problem may be caused by improper linkage adjustment, or worn synchronizers.

Automatic transmission

Many troubles can be traced to a low oil level, although a clogged filter can also make the unit misbehave. Beyond these basic problems, automatic transmission troubleshooting is complex and, again, would require a separate book. We can make the following points, however:

1. Gear changes are made by friction devices that hold one of the gears in the planetary gear set, while power is applied to another. The holding is performed by devices called bands, the power application by clutches (somewhat similar to the manual clutch). It is possible, up to a point, to adjust the bands to compensate for wearing off of the friction material; there is no adjustment for the clutches.

2. Sluggish acceleration below 30 to 35 mph and normal performance at higher speeds is usually caused by a defect in the torque converter, not the transmission.

3. The oil in the transmission has four jobs: to lubricate, to cool, to serve as a fluid under pressure to apply clutches and bands, and to operate the mechanical devices that regulate shifting. Therefore, it is good maintenance practice to have the transmission oil changed and the oil filter replaced at least every two years. On most cars, the bands can be inexpensively adjusted at the same time.

4. Sloppy shifting of the transmission is almost always caused by failure of one of two components that can be serviced without taking anything apart. One is the governor, a speed sensing device that transmits a type of shifting signal to the transmission. The other is the modulator, which responds to changes in engine intake manifold vacuum to contribute an opposing shifting signal to the transmission. It is the job of a body of valves inside the transmission to sort out the signals of these two components to decide when to shift.

DRIVESHAFT

Power is transferred from the transmission to the rear by a long shaft (called the driveshaft or propeller shaft), *See Fig. 40*. This shaft is not mounted straight and level, so it must be built with at least a couple of swivel joints (called universal joints) and if the car is long, a center support bearing.

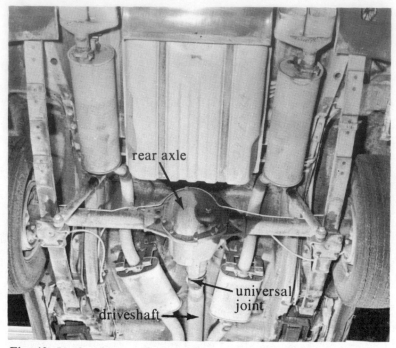

Fig. 40 *Under the car, the driveshaft, which begins at the rear of the transmission (not shown), goes to the rear axle. One of the driveshaft's two universal joints is visible.*

What Goes Wrong

In time, the universal joints wear. When they are worn to the point where there is a lot of free play in the parts, you may hear a clunking sound from underneath the car on acceleration. Worn universal joints must be replaced or they eventually will break apart. This would mean no connection between the transmission and the rear wheels, and the car wouldn't go.

REAR AXLE

The driveshaft connects to a miniature transmission (called the rear axle or differential) which changes the direction of the rotary motion of the driveshaft, and transmits it through short shafts (called axle shafts) to the rear wheels, *See Fig. 41*.

This little gearbox also has other functions:

1. It permits one wheel to turn faster than the other, which is necessary when you're turning a corner (the outer wheel has a greater distance to travel than the inside one, and without the differential, it would be dragged along, reducing tire life).

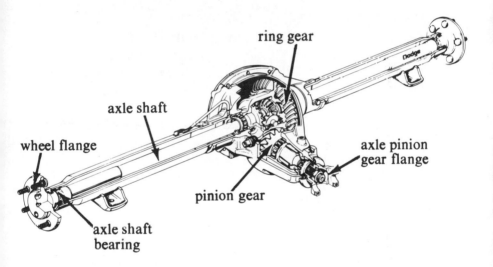

Fig. 41. *The rotating power from the driveshaft changes direction in the rear axle. The driveshaft is bolted to the axle pinion gear flange, so it turns the pinion gear. The pinion is in mesh with the ring gear so that the power direction is "bent" (refer back to Fig. 7 —bevel gears) to turn the rear wheels. The power is then carried by the axle shafts, which are supported in bearings in the rear axle. At the end of each axle shaft is a flange onto which the wheel is bolted. There are other gears in the rear axle, whose center section is called a differential, which allow the rear wheels to turn at different speeds when you go around corners.*

2. The rear axle provides a convenient place for a final speed reduction. This is usually about 3 to 1. That is, if the driveshaft is spinning at 900 revolutions per minute (rpm), the differential gears will reduce the speed to the tires to about 300 rpm.

First (or low) gear in a transmission also provides a 3 to 1 reduction in speed. This means that an engine turning at 2700 revolutions per minute will turn the rear wheels only 300 rpm, about 25 mph in the average car.

What Goes Wrong

The rear axle assembly is usually very reliable, and can be expected to last the life of the car. Occasionally, however, one of the oil seals fails and the unit must be taken apart. In the normal unit, some oil loss is inevitable and acceptable, but whenever you have the engine oil changed, make sure the man checks the oil level in the differential and adds oil as necessary.

A rare, but not totally uncommon, failure is of the bearings that support the axle shafts. When one bearing fails, only that one need be replaced.

BRAKING SYSTEM

When you step on the brake pedal, you start a chain of events that results in the pressing of slabs of friction material against smooth metal surfaces bolted to each wheel. The frictional force brings the wheels to a simultaneous stop.

The parts that have the friction material are called brake shoes, and the friction material itself is called brake lining.

The metal surfaces to which the wheels are bolted are called drums in one type of braking system, discs in another.

The drum looks like a cake pan, and the brake shoes are half-moon-shaped parts that are pushed against the inner side. The disc looks like a phonograph record and the brake shoes are flat pieces that are clamped against each flat side.

Regardless of the system, the brake shoes are applied by hydraulic pressure. Don't let this term panic you, for all it means is fluid under pressure and you work with that every time you turn on a faucet. In a braking system, the fluid is a special oil, and the system is filled with this oil and sealed.

Stepping on the pedal pushes a rod that pushes a piston in a small cylinder (called the brake master cylinder). At the end or side of the cylinder are two tubes, one that goes to the rear wheels, the other to the front wheels, *See Fig. 42.*

Fig. 42.   *This simple schematic shows the basic operation of a brake system that has discs in front and drums in the rear. When you step on the pedal, you transmit fluid under pressure through tubing to the brakes. In front, the pressure clamps friction material against both sides of a disc, using a clamping device called a caliper. In the rear, two little pistons in a wheel cylinder push curved sections of friction material against the inside surface of a cake-pan-shaped part called a drum. The special valves referred to are designed to make the combination of brake designs operate properly.*

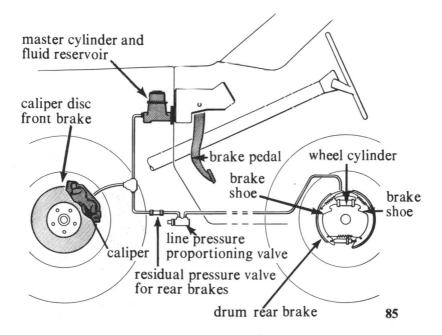

master cylinder and
fluid reservoir

caliper disc
front brake

brake pedal   wheel cylinder

brake
shoe

brake
shoe

caliper

line pressure
proportioning valve

residual pressure valve
for rear brakes

drum rear brake

Because the master cylinder and the tubing are filled with oil, the movement of the piston transfers your foot's pressure on the pedal through the oil-filled tubing. If this concept is hard to grasp, just realize that the water pressure you have at your faucet is created by a pumping station that may be miles away. When you open the faucet, the water under pressure pours out.

Cars with power brakes incorporate a unit operated by engine vacuum which provides assist to your foot in pushing the rod in the master cylinder. The vacuum assist doesn't improve the braking of the car—it just reduces the pedal pressure your foot has to supply.

The movement of the brake fluid through the oil-filled tubing from the master cylinder is transferred into the movement of smaller pistons that apply the brake shoes at the wheels. One of two devices is used:

1. In a drum braking system, *See Fig. 43 A,* there is another cylinder at each wheel (called the wheel cylinder) which has a piston at each end. The tubing from the master cylinder is connected into the middle of this cylinder, between the two pistons. The oil under pressure pushes the pistons outward, and a rod inserted into a recess in the outer face of each piston pushes the brake shoes against the inner circumference of the drum, *See Figs. 43 B and C.*

Fig. 43. *Here's a close-up look at the drum brake. Fig. 43 A shows the brake drum in place; Fig. 43 B, the brake drum's inside (with a wheel attached to the outside). This second photo has a finger pointing to the inner circumference, against which the brake shoes are pressed by the wheel cylinder pistons Fig. 43 C shows the key parts: steel brake shoe with asbestos friction material, the wheel cylinder with the little rods that push the brake shoe out when fluid pressure is applied to the pistons inside, and the shoe's automatic adjuster, which automatically moves the brake shoes outward a little bit at a time to compensate for wear on the friction material.*

brake drum   wheel bolts
on here

Fig. 43A

Fig. 43B

Fig. 43C

WHEEL CYLINDER

BRAKE SHOE

FRICTION MATERIAL

SHOE AUTOMATIC ADJUSTER

2. In the most popular type of disc braking system, there is a U-shaped clamp over the edge of the disc, *See Fig. 44 A.* When you step on the pedal, the oil under pressure pushes out a piston on one side of the caliper. As the piston pushes outward, it applies a flat brake shoe against one side of the disc. Simultaneously, the caliper slides along rods, and the piston's movement causes an equal and opposite reaction (Newton's law, you'll remember from high school science) on the caliper, pulling the other side toward the other side of the disc, *See Figs. 44 B and C.* A brake shoe is mounted on that side of the caliper and it is clamped against the other side of the disc.

Fig. 44. A   *This is the disc brake setup used on a Chevrolet Vega. The caliper has a single piston; when it pushes out (on the inside of the wheel), it presses one friction shoe against the inside of the disc and simultaneously draws the other side of the caliper (which slides along the rods) and its friction shoe against the outside of the disc. Fig. 44B shows the caliper removed from its position over the edge of the disc. You can see the flat brake shoes' friction material and the plastic guides of the caliper, through which the guide rods run. Fig. 44C shows the caliper with brake shoes removed. The single piston is visible.*

Fig. 44A

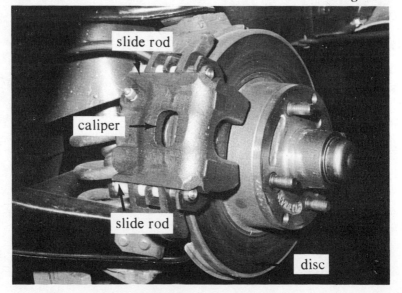

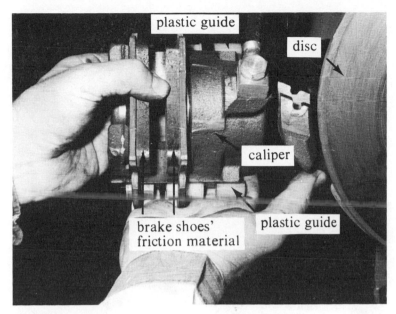

Fig. 44B

Fig. 44C

Most cars with disc brakes have them only on the front wheels, where 70 to 80 percent of the braking force is needed, to take advantage of the fact that the disc system is less subject to high-speed fading than drum types (heat causes brakes to fade, and the disc cools faster).

The drum brake, however, is superior for parking, and because the parking brake usually is just a manually operated linkage to the car's rear brakes, rarely a separate system, most cars still use drum brakes on the rear wheels.

With combination systems (drums in the rear, discs in front), a device called a metering valve must be used. This valve automatically compensates for the fact that the typical drum system shoes must overcome the pressure of springs before they can press against the drum.

What Goes Wrong

The most common work done on the brake system is replacement of the brake shoes with ones having a new friction lining. This is necessary every 20,000 miles on the average, although linings can wear out in as little as 5,000 miles or last for 40,000 miles or more. It all depends on how you drive and the overall operating conditions.

When you step on the brakes, your body lunges forward, and to a degree, so does some of the weight of the car. Stopping of forward momentum puts a greater strain on the front brakes, so they wear out faster. Rear brakes should last at least twice as long as front brakes, so don't automatically get the brakes at all four wheels serviced. Ask the mechanic to measure the thickness of the rear linings, and if all are at least 3/32-inch thick, they are fine.

The hydraulic system—master cylinder, tubing and hoses, and wheel cylinders or calipers—is subject to deterioration from the entry of dirt and water. This causes scratching and rusting of metal parts and failure of the little rubber seals that hold pressure in the master cylinder and wheel cylinders or calipers. If the brake pedal sinks to the floor under steady foot pressure, it means that the hydraulic system must be opened and these seals replaced. If the mechanic discovers fluid seeping from the wheel cylinders or calipers when he is replacing brake shoes, these units must be disassembled and the seals replaced. If there are deep scratches and/or heavy rusting, the parts must be replaced.

The wearing of the friction lining can cause deep scratches in the brake drum or disc. When this is found during lining replacement, the drum or disc may require resurfacing. Discs are tolerant of light scratches, however, and because they are more expensive to resurface than drums, the scratches can be safely ignored.

Other common brake problems are:

1. Brakes dragging. This is usually caused by a failure of the self-adjusting linkage on drum brakes. Sluggish release of the brakes, a form of dragging, also may be caused by defective brake shoe return springs (used only on drum brakes) and faulty adjustment of the brake master cylinder pushrod.
2. Brakes squealing. The usual cause is worn brake shoes, but some squealing can be considered normal on disc braking systems.
3. Brakes pulling. This indicates a failure of the brakes on one side of the car (the other side holds and pulls the car in its direction). The failure usually is caused by brake fluid or grease on the brake shoes, and for balanced braking you should replace the brake shoes on that side *and* the other side at the same time.

SUSPENSION AND STEERING

The suspension is a system of support for the frame of the car. It includes springs, which absorb road shocks, and the misnamed shock absorbers, which do not absorb shock but rather stop the springs from flexing up and down after they absorb the shocks.

The rear suspension is normally just a spring and a shock absorber at each wheel, but the front suspension consists of many components, for it also must accommodate the steering linkage.

The typical front suspension is shown in *Fig. 45.* The upper and lower control arms at each side are attached to

Fig. 45. *This coil spring front suspension is typical of all cars but those made by Chrysler Corporation, which uses a special type of spring called a torsion bar. The spring is between the upper and lower control arms, which are the connecting parts to the steering knuckle, on which the brakes and wheel are mounted in a bearing (so they can spin). The control arm connects with the knuckle by swivels called ball joints. The shock absorber (not visible here) is inside the coil-spring. The steering linkage also connects to the knuckle, so that when the knuckle is pivoted left or right, the wheel on it must follow.*

the frame at one end by a hingelike arrangement and to the steering knuckle by pivots (called ball joints) at the other end. The brake drum or disc is mounted on the knuckle in roller or ball bearings, and the wheel is bolted to a flange on the drum or disc, *See Fig. 46.*

The steering linkage pivots the steering knuckles and inasmuch as the drum or disc and wheel are mounted on the knuckles, they pivot when the knuckles do.

When you turn the steering wheel, you activate a gear and linkage system to pivot the knuckles. The steering wheel connects to a shaft that turns a gear in a little transmission (called a steering box). Your turning effort is transmitted from this box to linkage connected to components on which the wheels are mounted. On cars with power steering, a pump driven by the engine supplies oil under pressure to the steering box to assist the driver's turning effort.

Fig. 46. *This is a leaf spring rear suspension, in which the spring is composed of one or more long strips, though a coil spring setup is also widely used. In this photo, the lower part of the shock absorber can be seen.*

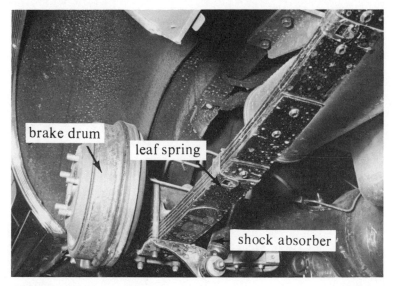

What Goes Wrong

Springs normally last the life of the car, but shock absorbers usually must be replaced every 25,000 miles. If the springs have sagged but not broken, you can install special shock absorbers that include an auxiliary spring to compensate for this.

Ball joints, when lubricated at least twice a year, last 50,000 to 100,000 miles depending on how lucky you are. If they're the lubricated-for-life type, you can still lubricate most of them, and increase their life. The so-called lifetime lubrication often doesn't work, and you find this out when the car is well out of warranty.

When ball joints wear, they impede steering and cause the car to shimmy. Many motorists find out about their car's ball joints when they take the car in for wheel alignment (a check and adjustment of the angles of various parts in the steering and front suspension system), and the mechanic says, "The ball joints are loose; I can't align the wheels." This discovery is accompanied by the shock of the price.

There is a less expensive way out: a resin that can be injected into the ball joint, where it hardens to compensate for wear. Made under the names "Lubri-Cast" and "Shimmy Stop" by 3M (the Scotch tape people), it costs less than half the price of replacement ball joints and is guaranteed for 25,000 miles. At this writing, most Goodyear tire stores and thousands of independent garages are offering the injections. A "Shimmy Stop" kit for weekend mechanics is available in discount houses, and we have seen men and women with little mechanical experience inject the resin without difficulty.

The bearings on which the wheel and brake drum or disc rotate should be removed and lubricated once a year, or they will eventually fail, causing a dangerous steering condition.

The steering linkage has little joints (called tierod ends). When these wear excessively, they cause looseness in the steering. Normally, they're good for 40,000 miles and up.

The steering linkage is braced by a pivoting link (called an idler arm). Its life is normally 50,000 miles and up, but units have been known to wear loose a lot sooner, and the result is an unstable feel to the steering.

TIRES

You might think that tires need no explanation—that every driver knows what they are. Fair enough, but there are details which few drivers understand.

There are three different types of tires in use today: bias-ply, belted bias-ply and radial. These terms describe different tire constructions—what's beneath the tread—which can affect ride, handling and wear.

1. Radial tires are the most expensive, but they last longest, are safer in high-speed driving, provide the best traction and improve gas mileage. Steel-belted radials are the longest lived of the radials, but fabric-belted radials ride better. Radials ride harsher than other designs at low speeds, and they cannot be mixed with other designs without causing possibly dangerous handling.

2. Belted bias-ply tires last longer than ordinary bias-ply tires and give better gas mileage, though not as good as radials. They can be mixed with bias-ply tires, which are the cheapest, and thus the type most popular as snow tires. The belts harshen the ride a bit, but not as much as the radial design.

3. Bias-ply tires are cheap in initial cost, but their short life makes them a sensible buy primarily for snow tires, which normally die of old age rather than wear, and for a car being nursed for less than a year before being sold, traded or junked.

Spend the money for your own tire gauge, and check pressures once a month. This is an investment in terms of economy and safety. Always keep the tires inflated to two to four pounds above the car maker's specifications. The ride won't be as silky smooth, but the car will handle better and the tires will last a lot longer. Service station gauges are as accurate as a thruway construction estimate, so always use your own gauge. The pressure should only be checked when tires are cool (car standing for four hours minimum, then driven no more than a couple of miles at low speed to a service station).

AIR CONDITIONING

Air conditioning is a system that relies on the use of a gas (called "Refrigerant 12") that boils at minus 22 degrees F or above, under atmospheric pressure. Under heavy pressure, however, it turns to a liquid.

A pumping device called a compressor is mounted on the engine and is pulley-driven by a belt from the crankshaft pulley. Other major components are: the condenser, a radiatorlike part mounted in front of the radiator; an expansion valve, which is a metering device for the gas; a receiver-dryer, which removes moisture from the gas; and an evaporator, *See Fig. 47.* This final part is what most people think of as the air conditioner, for it has the louvres and ducts and sits in the passenger compartment providing comfort. Actually the most significant part is a snake pit of tubes inside.

The air conditioning system is a sealed continuous loop. Let's begin at the compressor.

When you turn on the air conditioning, you close a switch to an electromagnet on the compressor. This joins the belt-driven pulley to the compressor, and starts the air conditioning cycle.

The compressor draws gas from the evaporator, compresses it and pumps it through the condenser. Because the condenser is mounted in front of the radiator, the fan draws air through it (as well as through the radiator). This cools the gas, and because it is under pressure from the compres-

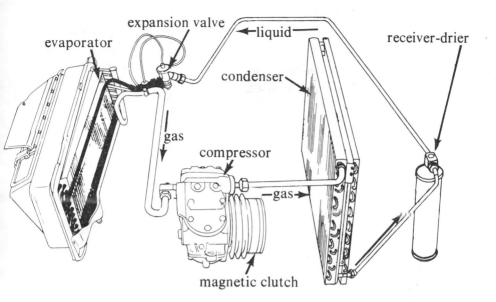

Fig. 47. *This drawing shows a typical air conditioning circuit. When the unit is turned on, a special refrigerant gas is circulated through the system by the compressor. The gas absorbs heat in the engine compartment and discharges it through the condenser, a radiator-like part mounted in front of the cooling system radiator. A little clear circular window on top of the receiver-dryer permits checking for loss of refrigerant gas, a major cause of performance problems.*

sor, it turns back to a liquid. The liquid flows through the receiver-dryer and then to the expansion valve. The valve restricts the flow, letting just enough get through so that the pressure is reduced. Lowering the pressure converts the liquid back to a boils-at-minus-22 gas.

When any liquid or gas boils, it absorbs heat, just as a pot of water on the stove absorbs heat from the burners. The refrigerant gas boils in the tubes of the evaporator, absorbing heat from the air surrounding the tubes. An electric fan, the blower, pushes the cooled air out into the passenger compartment.

What Goes Wrong

Air conditioning systems have many feet of tubes and hoses, and leaks may develop. When the refrigerant gas leaks out, the cooling performance of the unit drops. There is a little window (called a sight glass) into the sealed system on top of the receiver-dryer. If you turn on the unit and look into the glass, you'll see bubbles that should disappear in no more than about five minutes. If the bubbles persist, the air conditioning system needs a "recharge," that is, an addition of refrigerant gas. All air conditioners leak small amounts of refrigerant (there's no such thing as a perfect seal), and most units need a recharge after two to three years. If the unit suddenly drops in performance because of a gas loss, however, the leak is major and requires correction by a mechanic.

Every component in the air conditioning system can cause a performance drop or loss if it fails. Here are some checks you can make:

1. On a low-humidity, 80-degree day, turn on the unit and after it has been running for ten minutes, insert a thin thermometer into one of the louvre openings. Hold it there for a couple of minutes, then withdraw and after it has been running for ten minutes, insert a degrees less than the outside air temperature.
2. Check the sight glass for bubbles.
3. If the unit doesn't seem to be coming on at all, have someone turn on the switch while you watch the compressor pulley. If you don't hear a light click and/or see the pulley suddenly jerk (its instant magnetization to the compressor), the magnetic device, called a magnetic clutch, must be repaired.
4. Look for oil leakage at the compressor. If caught in time, it may be cured by inexpensive replacement of a

seal. Otherwise, the expensive compressor may have to be changed.

5. Press on the drive belt midway between compressor and crankshaft pulleys (engine off). The belt should deflect less than three-quarters of an inch under thumb pressure. A loose belt is an inexpensive-to-cure cause of poor performance, and a somewhat common one.

Air conditioning is an expensive-to-buy option that can also be extremely expensive to service if you have the automatic temperature control type. The automatic unit has a degree wheel—like a household thermostat—that turns on either heater or air conditioner to control the temperature. The automatic operation comes from a system of electronic and other controls that are expensive to fix or replace. If you avoid this design, sticking instead to the manually controlled type, you will still be warm in winter and cool in summer, and when the unit needs repair, the bite probably won't be as big.

CHAPTER 2

Determining Where the Problem Lies

The more you know and notice about your car and its problems, the better the information you can give to the shop that will do the repair work. Auto troubleshooting really involves educated guesswork and when the mechanic is faced with a problem that has many possible causes, he is obliged to keep testing until he turns up something wrong.

Some people believe that giving a mechanic very little information is the best way, on the theory that the mechanic will do a lot of checking and fix everything that's wrong, instead of just attending to an immediate problem.

Unfortunately, merely because something isn't right doesn't mean it's the cause of your complaint, and just because a part doesn't function according to manufacturer's specifications doesn't mean it will need replacement.

If you shortchange the mechanic on information, all you can be sure of are big bills.

To help the mechanic find your problem without extraneous and unnecessary work, you must understand what he needs to know about different types of problems. This chapter lists the most common problem areas, and the things you should notice and report. It's really a compilation of the questions a careful mechanic would like to ask if he got the chance.

ENGINE STARTING

Does the engine crank normally? (Cranking is that ugh, ugh, ugh turning sound when you hold the key in the start position.) Slow cranking should be obvious to any driver, and there is no such thing as an engine that cranks too fast. There is, however, the possibility that the starter is spinning, but not turning the engine. Do you hear a whirring sound, but none of the ugh, ugh, ugh of the engine turning?

Does the problem occur only when the engine is cold, only when hot, or only immediately following or during a heavy rainstorm?

Any sign of starting at all? Does it start for an instant and die as soon as you let go of the key? Do you have to pump the gas pedal to get any sign of starting, or perhaps hold the pedal to the floor?

ENGINE STALLING

Does the engine restart easily after any or all of the stalling situations? Is a special technique required, such as pumping the gas pedal or holding it to the floor?

Do you get the stall on acceleration, deceleration, hard braking or when you're just sitting, perhaps at a traffic light? Does it happen only when the engine is cold, or only when hot, or right after or during a heavy rainstorm?

ENGINE OVERHEATING

How do you know it's overheating—steam pouring out, warning light or gauge reading? Does the problem only occur in heavy traffic, or sitting at idle? Does the gauge always read high, or does it suddenly rise sharply? And when? What was the date of the last cooling system drain and flush?

POOR ENGINE PERFORMANCE

Is the problem failure to reach certain speeds, lack of acceleration or inability to climb hills? If it's acceleration, is it only at low speed, only at high speed, or at all speeds?

POOR GAS MILEAGE

If you just bring your car in and complain of poor gas mileage, the mechanic may simply recommend a major tune-up and that's it. Before you waste money unnecessarily, perform an accurate test to determine gas mileage.

Fill the tank to the absolute top, note the exact mileage on the speedometer's mileage indicator (to the tenth of a mile) and take a 50-mile run one way, then back, on a super-highway at a steady 45 to 50 mph. Go back to the same station, fill up again—from the same pump with the car facing the same way.

Record the exact amount of gas necessary to fill up (to the tenth of a gallon), and divide the distance traveled. You may discover that your mileage isn't bad at all, in which case what you felt was poor gas mileage may have been caused by operating conditions (lots of stop and go, hard acceleration, uneven speeds).

If you're still dissatisfied with the mileage, take the car to the shop, describe what you did and what the mileage was. Also notice if you smell gas from under the hood, or if you see any seepage from the gas tank.

TRANSMISSION PROBLEM

Manual transmission: Hear a noise? Is it metallic? Any trouble shifting? Into what gear? Transmission lever jumps out of gear? What gear? Only at certain speeds or at any speed? Or does the engine seem to be racing when the car isn't going very fast (apparent slippage of the clutch friction disc)?

Automatic transmission: Strange noises like moans and groans? Any accompanying problems, such as poor acceleration, temporary loss of drive when you first start moving? When was the last time the oil and filter were changed?

Poor shifting? Does transmission seem to upshift at too low a speed, or too high a speed, or not at all? Or doesn't it seem to downshift when your road speed drops? Or is the shifting very rough, clunking into gear? When were the bands adjusted last, if ever?

BRAKES

Squealing noises? Throbbing in the brake petal as you apply the brakes? Pulling to one side? Which one? Or is the problem caused by the rear end of the car swerving on braking?

Brake fade? What do you mean—brakes lose holding power stopping from high speed or pedal sinks to the floor under heavy braking with noticeable loss of braking effectiveness?

POOR RIDE

On what kind of roads? Would a road test help show the mechanic exactly what you mean?

VIBRATION, NOISES, SHAKE

At what road speed, or on acceleration, or deceleration, or braking? Does it occur on all kinds of roads? If not, on what kinds? Does the problem occur if you put the gearshift lever in neutral and coast? Again, would a road test help show the mechanic exactly what you mean?

HANDLING AND STEERING

Looseness or shake as you enter turns? Or does the car veer uncontrollably some of the time? Do you always have the brakes on when the problem occurs? A road test is probably necessary to show the mechanic exactly what you mean.

CHAPTER 3

The Types of Shops and Picking the One That's Right for You

As recently as fifteen or twenty years ago, cars still were sufficiently uncomplicated for a car owner to rely on one good general repair garage for all of his or her needs. Today, no shop does everything, and the owner must patronize a number of shops.

Even the car dealership, which is normally obligated to accept any job on a make of car it sells, doesn't do everything. It sends many jobs to specialty shops, particularly body work and upholstery, and may even send overflow work to one of the other types of shops listed in this chapter. In any case, the car dealership is so much more expensive than most other types of shops that you should avoid it where possible.

Knowing where to go for a particular problem is half the battle in getting good work at fair prices. You could try driving into a shop that advertises "General Auto Repairs," but you'd soon find that the term "general" is a misnomer, and the shop really is limited to a certain category or level of work. Even if it offers to do the work you need, it may be the most expensive or least qualified choice.

How can you determine where to go? You might think you could find out what's wrong with the car by driving into one of these "diagnostic centers" which offer you "electronic computerized analysis." However, there are few of these centers, and those that do exist are fighting a battle for survival. Most people are not willing to pay the rather high inspection charges when the car is running, and when it isn't (or is just sputtering along), they want to get it to the right kind of shop as quickly as possible.

Diagnostic centers are often very impressive-looking operations, but as we will explain later, they are really of no help to the woman looking for a good, unbiased opinion. Your best approach is to pick a suitable shop based on your own general evaluation of the problem.

"Good grief, does this mean I have to learn how auto repairs are done?" No, it doesn't. The difference between learning auto mechanics and being an informed customer is substantial. You don't have to know *how* to do a repair job to understand *what* must be done and *where*.

Many car problems just require common sense. If your car doesn't start, you don't call a shop that advertises itself as a brake or air conditioning specialist.

Then, if you take the time to learn the basics of the different systems in your car (see Chapter 1), you'll make the right decisions almost all the time. Unfortunately, no one shop can solve all of your automotive problems. Your car may need work that requires special skills or is most economically performed by a specialist, or you may need service on a Sunday, when the shop you normally patronize is closed. Even more difficult, you may have to find a shop far from home. And it's not unlikely that the shop you were satisfied with last year may change for the worse.

An automobile is a large investment, and you should give the selection of repair shops even more thought than you give the choice of other retail shops you patronize. Here are the types of shops from which to choose:

CAR DEALER

Many women like the impersonality of the large car dealership. Its antiseptic waiting room and the amiable men who write up the repair order present a less threatening atmosphere than the smaller shop. Unhappily, the prices are very high, and you may have to wait three weeks for an appointment, or your car may sit there for weeks waiting for parts to arrive. The quality of work is often reasonably good, provided that you have been very specific about your car's problem. If you haven't, you may find that the job hasn't been done right, or that it hasn't been done at all. Those friendly men are service salesmen, and although they're glib, they usually don't know much more about cars than you do. They normally work on commission and may try to sell you everything under the sun. Their advantage is that few people expect to have to muster sales resistance in a service shop.

Additionally, their repair orders, unless you are specific, may be written so vaguely that they constitute a carte blanche for the mechanic, and a huge repair bill for you.

You should only consider the car dealer—large or small—if you have a problem with a car under warranty, or if there is difficulty with one of these complex accessories: power seats, speed control, power windows, power door locks or perhaps air conditioning of the automatic temperature control type. The car dealer is about 30 percent more expensive than a quality independent shop, but on these jobs he is more likely to have a specialist who is really familiar with the systems.

There are many reasons why the dealer is more expensive. For one, he must make a lower profit or even take a loss on warranty work, which is made up by charging the retail customer more.

Second, he installs only parts supplied by the car manufacturer, which are more expensive, although no better, than those available from quality independent manufacturers. The independent shop, by contrast, buys from a variety of sources, including, when appropriate, wrecking yards, and may be able to obtain just-as-good components for half the price of those from the car manufacturer. The dealer's frequent "wait for parts from Detroit" is a common reason why cars sit in these shops so long.

Finally, unionization is more prevalent among car

dealers than independent shops, and union mechanics' wage rates are higher.

INDEPENDENT GARAGE

The typical independent garage presents a less attractive atmosphere, but it is the best overall choice for most medium-to-heavy repairs. The prices are lower than the dealer's, and the quality of work is as good and often better. The prices aren't cheap, however, and for some jobs in the medium-to-heavy category, you can get work that is as satisfactory, for measurably less, at other types of shops.

The independent shops normally do not do every type of repair job and in fact are much more limited than the car dealer. They often advertise "General Auto Repairs" or even "Complete Auto Repairs," but actually perform only the types of work most commonly needed, such as:

1. engine tuneup
2. brakes
3. starting and charging systems
4. lights and horns
5. suspension (shock absorbers, springs and ball joints)
6. steering
7. manual clutch
8. exhaust system
9. some engine services, but stopping well short of complete overhaul.

The independent garage's advantage is that it is run by the proprietor. In a car dealership, the owner is more concerned with sales than service.

The independent garage operator can make a handsome living with satisfied customers, so he is likely to check and double-check his men very carefully. He is always a mechanic and usually the best one in the shop. The quality of the shop's work often suffers, therefore, if he is on vacation or has built such a large operation that he cannot exercise tight control.

SERVICE STATION

The gasoline service station is convenient, open long hours and is a place where you can feel at ease. Usually after just a few weeks of gasoline purchases, the faces and perhaps even the names of the men who work there are familiar, and you will be known to them.

Service stations, however, are normally limited to quick light-to-medium repairs—jobs that can be done in two hours or less. There are exceptions, but the typical service station operator is discouraged from doing other than quick jobs by the oil company that supplies him. The object is to keep the service bays from being tied up so that the station can concentrate on selling the oil company's products, which include car lubricants.

Even if the station has a sign that says, "Mechanic on Duty," or "General Auto Repairs," it normally limits itself to no more than the following, which are in the light-to-medium category:

1. engine tuneup
2. brakes
3. shock absorbers
4. exhaust system
5. tire and battery installations
6. tire and battery service
7. lubrication and replacement of engine filters
8. replacement of headlamps, bulbs and windshield wiper blades.

Many service stations will accept almost any job, but send it out to an independent garage which does the job and gives the station operator a commission. The commission normally doesn't raise the price of the work to you, but in some cases it may.

Most of the men who work in stations are not mechanics, but have been trained to do specific jobs. Because most of the work is not done by mechanics, it is far less expensive than comparable work in car dealerships or independent garages. Even those jobs that are done by a service station mechanic are cheaper, because the station is set up to do them expeditiously.

DIAGNOSTIC CENTER

At one time, the diagnostic center was hailed as the place where the public could obtain unbiased opinions furnished by an impartial computerized electronic test center.

The mass of flashing lights, automatic printouts of reports and even "magic wands" that, when waved over an engine, performed a diagnosis that was translated into the printed report—all of this was very impressive.

Unfortunately, it was largely show business to impress the gullible. Much of the printed report was based on a mechanic's inspection, and it was therefore no better, no more accurate, than the man making the checks. There is a very sharp limit to what unaided test equipment can tell.

There are some diagnostic centers still in operation, but most of them offer repair work to stay in business, thereby losing their impartial image. If you take your car into such a center, you may find that the printed report lists dozens of alleged defects in a car that is basically running well. Very often a part will not meet certain test standards, but this doesn't mean that it requires replacement.

Probably the worst problem the diagnosis-only center faces is that most people are unwilling to spend $10 to $20 to have a car checked out if it's running decently. Except for some obvious items in the mechanic's visual inspection (such as oil leaks), there is little a diagnostic center can tell you about a car that's running well, insofar as early future trouble is concerned.

Most car dealers and quality independent garages have far less expensive versions of the diagnostic center's equipment—no wands or flashing lights, just what is necessary for analysis—and they have the mechanics too. The result is that the diagnostic center with repair facilities is nothing more than an expensive version of the independent garage.

SPECIALTY SHOP

As auto repair became more complex, it was only natural that specialists would come on the scene. Some of the specialists are quite familiar to most drivers, namely the franchised shops that do brakes, tuneup, automatic transmissions, exhaust system and suspension service. They advertise heavily, promoting their alleged expertise and courteous and fair treatment.

The specialty shop has its advantages and disadvantages. The main advantage is that by specializing it can offer some degree of competence in what it does. Also, if the part is a commonly replaced one, such as the muffler, it can offer lower prices because of its high volume. The specialty shop also may be able to train nonmechanics for certain functions, pay them less and pass part of the wage saving along to you.

The disadvantage is that the specialist sees you once a year or less. As a result, all too many specialists tend to oversell, working on a "get them while the getting is good" theory.

Franchised shops are the worst offenders. They don't rely on satisfied customers telling friends, but instead on the drawing power of national advertising.

In all too many cases, they try to sell you the job on which they make the most profit, whether you really need it or not. The franchised automatic transmission shops are in business to install completely rebuilt units, not to perform minor repairs. The brake shops make their money on complete brake jobs, not the basic job that is sufficient for most cars. Someone has to pay for the franchising fees, the ad budgets and, in some cases, for absentee ownership.

Many franchised shops are absolute artists when it comes to selling. They have neat waiting rooms, perhaps with copies of popular magazines and a free coffee bar. You are attended by a neat, friendly man in a white coat, very much like the man in the big car dealership—long on charm but short on technical know-how. Selling is his forte, and most people are sold on the "security" of a complete brake job, rebuilt automatic transmission, or an engine tuneup that "won't put you in trouble at 60 mph on the thruway."

If you need work that must be entrusted to a specialist, such as air conditioning service, engine overhaul or automatic transmission service, you will do better at an independent specialty shop.

This shop is usually an ex-independent garage that decided to "go specialty," generally a decision based on the owner's personal preference in repair work. The advertising is limited to the yellow pages, so the shop must rely on satisfied customers and lower prices to compete with the franchised operations. The independent specialist may not provide the cheerful waiting room, but he could save you a lot of money.

OTHER TYPES OF SHOPS

There are many types of limited-service shops in operation, most of which are specialty shops of a sort. These include:

1. Auto repair centers built into department stores or discount houses.
2. Repair facilities in tire dealers.
3. Service shops in retail home-and-auto supply stores.

These shops provide a few of the basic jobs in the service station category—light-to-medium repairs. The men are specially trained nonmechanics, and although the prices are lower than many stations', you should have a reasonable idea of the work you need before you consider them. If you can hear the sound of a defective muffler, or have had your battery tested and know it is defective, these shops can save you quite a bit of money, particularly if you need the work when they are having a sale.

These shops also can be reasonably priced and quite satisfactory for a routine brake job. Most people consider brake work to be highly sophisticated, requiring the services of a master mechanic. Actually, it's the kind of work that can be taught to a nonmechanic very successfully.

You should only go to this type of shop if you have no unusual brake problems, such as pedal pulsations, brake pulling or grabbing, failure of the power assist, and strange noises (other than light squealing) on brake application. All you want is to restore brakes that just aren't stopping the car as well as they once did, and you have some indication that the problem is normal wear (such as a 15,000-mile or greater interval since the last brake job). Special problems should be brought to an independent garage, which may find they are not in the brake system at all.

The limited-service shop of this type is at its weakest when it attempts to do other than simple installations. If you have a problem you want someone to troubleshoot, these shops aren't a good choice. Tuneup is another of their weak jobs. They can successfully handle something like a prevacation tuneup—in which certain parts are replaced as a form of insurance—but don't trust them with a tuneup in which you expect a specific performance problem to be solved.

THE PART-TIME BACKYARD SHOP

The man who runs a little auto repair shop part time in his backyard still is found in many parts of the country, but he is a poor choice for almost any kind of repair work.

It's difficult enough to do decent repair work on today's cars in a full-time properly equipped shop, and the part-timer working in his backyard usually has neither the equipment nor the know-how. He draws his customers from the immediate area with low price quotes, but even if he's a friendly next-door neighbor, take your business elsewhere.

How do you decide which of these shops is right for you?

A REGULAR SHOP

Your choice of a shop for most routine work should be limited to a service station or independent garage. You could patronize a car dealership, but high prices and long waits for appointments should be enough to convince all but the most stubborn to avoid them when possible.

Begin the search by asking friends for recommendations, with this one stipulation: if you have a foreign car, only ask friends with foreign cars. Some shops either do not service imports or handle so few of them that they cannot do good work at reasonable prices.

Look for a shop that is a member of the Independent Garage Owners of America, the leading trade association. IGOA shops are a bit more expensive than the competition, but they're usually among the best and worth the extra money. IGOA shops normally will have the association emblem prominently displayed. Note: you won't find an IGOA shop everywhere, for the association is not organized in several states and in some others has only a few members.

Before patronizing a shop, make a quick inspection, checking the following points:

1. Is the shop clean at the beginning of the workday (a shop that wasn't cleaned when it closed for business the night before is hardly ready for an efficient day's work)?
2. Are there any current reference books in view, such as Motor's or Chilton's auto repair manuals (fixing today's cars demands periodic reference to such manuals)?

3. Does the shop have test equipment, the most important being a reasonably sized oscilloscope? It takes good equipment to do accurate work on today's cars.

4. Is the shop usually busy? Even a good shop can have a slow week or two, but the shop that never seems to have much work probably doesn't deserve it.

5. Does the shop have at least two full-time men? A one-man shop just can't function efficiently. The man can't go out for parts when necessary without closing his doors. He may take twice as long to do certain jobs because a second pair of hands isn't around to help. His overhead must be borne only by him, which raises his hourly costs.

TRYING OUT THE SHOP

If a shop appears to be promising, don't wait for an emergency to try it out. Your car needs an engine oil and filter change at least twice a year, perhaps more often, and possibly a chassis lubrication.

Make an appointment for a time that will permit the shop to do the job while you wait, and while you're waiting, watch. A shop may not allow customers in the work area but, in all but very large car dealerships, there's always some location from which you can see the man working.

A conscientious man doing an engine oil change should also check the lubricant in the rear axle of the car and the transmission. It's a very good sign if he also checks the battery water and the brake fluid level.

If the chassis is being lubricated, make sure he wipes road film off the grease fittings (the nipples into which the grease is injected with a gun). Note: some cars do not have fittings, only little plugs which the man must remove, installing grease fittings in their place to lubricate the chassis. In this case, the grease fittings are clean and do not have to be wiped off.

Don't decide to patronize a shop just because the

owner seems to be treating you with a reasonable amount of respect if the shop falls short of the qualities outlined earlier. Unfortunately, there's no correlation between good work and good manners. A woman usually gets respect only by displaying an intelligent awareness of her car and its needs. On the other hand, don't continue to patronize a shop where intelligent awareness on your part doesn't improve the personnel's treatment. Good work and reasonable manners are not mutually exclusive qualities either.

Service stations tend to be somewhat friendlier toward women than independent garages, simply because they see them on a regular basis for gasoline. However, most stations do such a limited range of work that you will have to patronize an independent garage in addition.

SPECIALTY WORK

A specialty shop can be a good place to go for work when you know what's wrong. The putt-putt sound of a hole in the exhaust system, or the erratic performance of the automatic transmission, is very obvious, and the services of a specialty shop can save you time and perhaps some money.

The exhaust system specialty shop that is part of a department store, discount house or tire dealer can save you up to 30 percent over a station or garage, particularly if it has a sale going on. The chain muffler shops are not that much cheaper than service stations, unless they have an inexpensive line of parts for sale, and these second lines are strictly for the car you plan to keep no more than a year or so.

The choice of an automatic transmission specialist is not easy. Because of high prices and overselling by so many, the franchised shops should be a last resort. The independent shops are few and far between, and listed only in the yellow pages. If you can get a recommendation or find one that looks clean and busy, you're ahead. As your car accumulates mileage and needs some basic transmission maintenance (such as an oil and filter change), give such a shop a try and look it over. If you see some of the men doing work without removing the transmission, that's a good sign. It hopefully means that the shop does repairs when possible, rather than sell overhauled transmissions to everyone.

Brake specialists are plentiful, and for good reason—brake work isn't that difficult to do right, and even a non-mechanic can be trained to do it rather easily. If the brakes are just starting to squeal, but the pedal is reasonably firm, odds are that all you need are new brake shoes. If the pedal sinks to the floor under steady foot pressure, more involved work is probably needed. Either of these common conditions, however, can easily be handled by the less expensive shops that do brake and exhaust system service, such as those in discount houses, department stores and tire dealerships.

If the pedal doesn't sink to the floor, however, be wary of the shop that insists on selling you a complete overhaul. You'll be getting work you don't need.

Air conditioning specialists are either independent garages that do some general work (to keep going all year round) or radiator shops that have tacked on this specialty. There are many specialists who are over matched trying to service automatic temperature control systems, which are best left to car dealers. If you'd prefer to try an independent, however, look for the NARSA emblem (radiator repairman's association), which provides members with necessary technical data.

Note: service stations that advertise "Complete Air Conditioning Service" usually don't perform it. They do only the common and simple maintenance and minor repairs.

EMERGENCY NEAR HOME

If you patronize a station or independent garage and are satisfied, leave the car where it is or have it towed to the shop when an emergency occurs. Trying to get a car fixed late at night or on Sundays usually is futile, for the only places that are open are service stations, and the mechanic, if there is one, isn't on duty. Service station attendants may try to be helpful, but they are usually short on knowledge, even if long on technical talk.

About the only common emergency jobs you can have done by a station attendant (and you'll have to lift the hood to see what the problem is) are the following: radiator hose, fan or power steering belt, flat tire, burned out headlamp, blown fuse and possibly a stuck horn button (you've got no choice when the horns are blowing: you must get something done).

EMERGENCY FAR FROM HOME

There's no worse feeling than an emergency when you are many miles from home. You have to take action, and there's little chance for reflection, no opportunity to inspect shops and check prices.

The techniques for finding a qualified shop are not hard and fast. If a car dealer is nearby, it's a possibility—if he can take your car and get to work on it immediately. The price will be high, but at least you've got some assurance of competence.

Sometimes telephone operators will prove helpful, and more than one stranded motorist has enlisted the aid of a local minister.

Local police departments can also be helpful, although some will do no more than call the nearest 24-hour towing service to get your car off the road. The towing service driver is never a mechanic.

Any of these approaches, however, is better than just looking for the nearest shop or panicking. A car is just a machine and no matter where it gives trouble, you'll do better by staying calm and trying to get competent help, even if it delays a trip by a day or two.

AVOIDING THE CHEATS

Fortunately, most men in the auto repair field are honest, which is truly remarkable when one considers that the field is not high paying and the opportunities to cheat without being caught are excellent.

A major factor contributing to honesty is that any shop that is reasonably competent will enjoy a high volume of work. The owner of a quality shop can earn a decent (if not spectacular) living just by turning out the work that needs doing. Unfortunately, there are some shop owners that think they can get rich by cheating and, unhappily, a few succeed.

Surprisingly, you are least likely to be sold unnecessary work when you have a road emergency far from home. In this case, your car is an unexpected intruder in the shop, and the operator wants to get you on your way as fast as possible. He may install a major component, rather than take the time to repair, but he is not too likely to spend time doing work that is totally superfluous.

Although honesty is prevalent, a woman has to be on her guard for two reasons:

1. Women are more likely to be cheated because a shop assumes they don't know anything about auto repair.
2. Women are more likely to be oversold, usually quite honestly, because the shop owner believes he knows what's best for a woman—without even discussing the subject with you. Yes, it's male chauvinism pure and simple.

The worst out-and-out cheats are "last-chance" gas stations on secondary roads. In such stations, tires may be slashed and other tricks may be tried, particularly on a woman. If you are traveling alone, never leave your car unguarded if you must stop for gas. Your best choice is to fill the tank and have the oil checked in a busy highway station and avoid the last-chance operations altogether. If you must stop for personal needs, pick a busy diner.

No matter where you go for gas, however, beware of the scare tactics that the gyps employ. They can have the unwary believing that the car will never get a mile away unless an emergency repair is made immediately. One popular technique is to squirt some oil under the car and tell you the engine is leaking and will explode unless the leak is fixed.

If your car has been running normally, you can check the engine and transmission oil levels yourself to see if they're correct. Just remember, a leak will show up as a trail of oil from the station driveway to where your car is stopped, not just a pool under the car.

Another common ploy is to take out the air filter element, show the motorist how dirty it is and warn him or her that unless a clean new filter is purchased immediately, the engine will be ruined. The fact is, a dirty air filter element should be replaced (primarily for better gas mileage), but there's absolutely no panic about it. The job is very easy and you can do it yourself at a substantial saving over the filter's list-price-plus-installation-cost (or the possibly inflated price quoted by the scare artist). Unnecessary scare tactics should not be rewarded by a purchase, and even if you want to get someone to do the job, pick another station. The honest station that checks your air filter will also give you a comparison look between clean and dirty filter elements, and simply suggest replacement for better gas mileage.

Before you leave on a long trip, always get your car inspected by your regular shop. This will not only provide reasonable assurance of a breakdown-free trip, but will give you the confidence to drive away from the scare specialists.

CHEATS NEAR HOME

Most of your maintenance and repair work is done near home, so you also face some risk of being cheated in your own neighborhood. A station doesn't have to be a last-chance operation to pull a scare tactic.

If you avoid the franchised specialist, where you are more likely to be oversold, you eliminate much of the risk of being taken on expensive jobs. For example, a $300 rebuilt automatic transmission may solve a problem of erratic shifting, but so might a $12 part called a modulator that can be installed in two minutes. A $150 brake job may give you a car that stops, but the same result might be obtained for $35 or $40.

There is no way to avoid paying for work done unnecessarily because of faulty diagnosis. Mechanics make mistakes and, like doctors, they charge for them. Is this dishonesty? Perhaps, but just think about the day on the job when you did everything wrong and still collected full pay for the week.

CHAPTER 4 | Dealing with the Shop

Except in the very small repair shops and some service stations, you will usually not deal directly with the mechanic when you take your car in for service. In very large car dealerships, you may not even see the mechanic.

You normally must work out the details with the man who takes your order, whether he's a service salesman in a car dealership or in a franchised specialty shop, or the owner or manager of an independent garage or service station.

In many cases, you have no real idea of what must be done. Whether you're crystal clear or vague, however, you'll be asked to sign a repair order, which is a legal obligation to pay for work ordered. If you refuse to pay, the shop can hold your car and eventually sell it, under a legal sanction referred to as a "mechanic's lien." Therefore, you should know what you're agreeing to.

Be as specific as you can about what's wrong. Chapters 1 and 2 should give you the know-how to reasonably isolate the problem. If you have several problems you want fixed, make up a typewritten list and keep a copy. That list should contain all the applicable information. For example:

"1. Car hard to start when cold unless I keep flooring the gas pedal while cranking it. Once it starts, it immediately stalls several times.

"2. Oil pressure warning light occasionally comes on bright. It goes off just as suddenly as it comes on. This

121

can happen when the engine is cold, warm, at 60 mph or when I'm stopped for a light, or it may not happen at all.

"3. Air conditioning works fine for first 10 or 15 minutes, then starts blowing warm air. If I turn it off for a few hours, and then back on, it works again for 10 to 15 minutes."

Contrast that with a list that reads:

"1. Car hard to start."
"2. Oil warning light keeps coming on."
"3. Air conditioning doesn't work properly."

In the first list, the mechanic has all the information he needs to go right to work, and with little wasted motion. The second list is so vague that a mechanic literally could spend hours trying to duplicate your problems in order to troubleshoot them. In cases of the first two items, he might never be able to make a diagnosis. You'd be charged for his hours of checkout, and no corrective work would have been done.

The first problem, for example, is almost certainly in the automatic choke. Without the information in the first list, a mechanic probably would perform a major tuneup, which might or might not include automatic choke service (each shop has its own definition of a major tuneup). The bill easily could run to $100 or more, compared with as little as $3 for an automatic choke adjustment and perhaps $10 to $15 more if the choke must be replaced.

The mechanic working from the second list would do all the extra work because he would have no other way to know where your problem is. He would make the assumption that a major tuneup would cure the difficulty, even if it includes superfluous services and parts. This is a very common procedure in shops where a clear-cut definition of the customer's problem has not been obtained, and the difficulty is not readily apparent.

ADVANCE ESTIMATES AND CALL LIMITS

Most repair jobs are obvious to the shop after a brief checkout, and you should wait at the shop until you can find out what the difficulty is and what the price is likely to be. The shop should be able to give you a very close estimate on most jobs, because labor prices are based on flat-rate charges. That is, you will be charged a specific amount for a particular job on your car (or any other car of the same make, model and year) no matter how long it takes or how quickly it is done. The charges are based on time studies for average mechanics as published in a reference manual. So although you may "overpay" if a fast mechanic finishes the job quickly, you gain if a slower man takes a great deal of time or if there is an unexpected difficulty with a rusty nut or bolt.

Although virtually all shops base their labor charges on flat rates, the final prices aren't the same for two reasons: (1) The flat rate is only a time (such as two hours to do a basic brake job) and each shop has a different hourly labor price. A shop that charges $8 per hour will ask $16 labor for the brake job; one that charges $12 per hour will get $24. (2) The prices of parts are not necessarily uniform. Some shops only install new parts; others will install rebuilt components they trust, and rebuilts are much less expensive. In general, new car dealers install new parts, independent garages and service stations use both new and rebuilt, and in some cases, parts procured from wrecking yards (which are even less expensive than rebuilt units).

If you want to check the fairness of a shop's price estimate, buy one of the consumer car repair price guides available at newsstands and book stores for about $1.50 to $2. The better guides cover the prices for parts and labor for common repairs, and give you information on typical rates for mechanic's labor in different parts of the country. Labor rates vary widely throughout the country, and what looks like a bargain in San Francisco would be considered outright robbery in rural Arkansas.

Some jobs cannot be checked out quickly and estimated on the spot. When you must leave your car without an estimate on the bill, ask the man who is writing your order to put a "call limit" on it, that is, a maximum amount you authorize for repair. If they later determine that the work necessary is likely to exceed the amount authorized by more than a few dollars, you will be called before the shop proceeds.

How much you should specify as a call limit depends on the individual situation. Examples:

You are told that the problem could either be something very minor and cost $10 to fix or something very major that could run $150 or more. Put a call limit of $10 on the job. If the problem is big, it should be contemplated very carefully. Perhaps there is, after all, a less expensive way out. Or you may want to invest more money to insure a job that will really last. Your decision should largely be based on how much additional life you can realistically expect from the car. As a rule of thumb, you should not invest more than half the wholesale value of the car in a major repair or group of repairs.

You are told that the repair could cost anywhere from $60 to $100. Assuming the repair is not elective (something that can be put off, such as a stuck power window or seat, door lock, radio, etc.), you will either have the work done or dispose of the car. If the $100 figure is no more than half the wholesale value of the car, set a $100 limit.

Jobs that are difficult for the shop to estimate are those that involve some guesswork and lots of checking, such as: finding a rattle or vibration, tracing an electrical short circuit, pinpointing causes of uncomfortable ride or poor handling, and determining the cause of some types of engine stalling. In these cases, you may have to pay for a couple of hours or more of inspection and testing, and in some big-city shops, that can be quite expensive. If a shop cannot give you an estimate without extensive investment in labor time, you may be able to live with the problem, particularly if it's only a rattle or vibration.

REBUILT AND WRECKING YARD PARTS

Once a problem has been isolated, you probably want it fixed—but not at any price. There are many ways a shop can save you money, but it may not offer you a choice unless you ask for one. One of the most common ways you can save is by installation of a part overhauled by a remanufacturer or one from a late-model wrecked car. Many drivers feel safer with new parts, but consider this: a new part can easily be defective (you've heard about the recalls by the car makers to replace new parts that aren't working so well). A rebuilt part, if nothing else, has been checked out for proper performance. And a wrecking yard part actually worked on someone's car and will be tested before installation in your car.

The airlines, which must meet strict government safety standards, use retreaded tires and rebuilt components for landing gear wheels.

In an automobile, some rebuilt or wrecking yard parts aren't worth the effort of obtaining them. This is primarily true when the new part is relatively inexpensive ($15 or less) or when its removal from a wrecked car is time consuming. Additionally, some parts just don't lend themselves to economical rebuilding.

Another consideration is that most shops don't want to bother looking for a part in a wrecking yard—no matter what the saving—if it is available in new or rebuilt form from their regular sources of supply, which usually offer fast and free delivery. If you can save substantially with a wrecking yard part, you may have to get it yourself, calling wreckers (listed in the yellow pages) until you find one that has it. Then you'll have to find a friend with a car (assuming yours doesn't run safely) to go with you to get it.

Women customers are not routine at wrecking yards— but why be bashful when there's a chance to save money? The repair shop will charge you a bit more to install a wrecking yard part on which it makes no profit, but you will still be ahead.

Note: some repair shops will flatly refuse to install a wrecking yard part they didn't themselves obtain, so determine if you can get the mechanic to do the job before you make your search.

Here are the jobs in which rebuilt or wrecking yard parts are a sensible choice:

Generator, Starter or Windshield Wiper Motor: Rebuilts are 40 to 60 percent cheaper than new parts, and wrecking yard units are still less expensive, by another 25 percent. Most shops, however, can obtain rebuilts easily, and will be reluctant to install a wrecking yard part.

Brakes: Used brake shoes relined with new friction material are up to 70 percent cheaper than brand new brake shoes, and when a quality friction material is applied they are just as good. If the brakes are of the drum type, and a drum is defective and cannot be serviced, you could ask for a used drum from a wrecking yard. Even if the wrecking yard drum requires service, the cost will be far less than that of a new one. A shop may be unwilling to accept a used drum if only one is defective, but if two require replacement, it should accept wrecking yard parts. If it is unwilling, find another shop for the next job you need.

Water Pump: A rebuilt is about half the price of a new unit and is just as good.

Carburetor: A rebuilt carburetor is 40 to 70 percent less expensive than a new one, and although there are minor advantages to the new unit, they do not justify the cost difference.

Ignition Distributor: A rebuilt saves you at least 30 percent with no loss in reliability.

Power Steering: Rebuilt power steering pumps and gearboxes are a sensible choice and provide a 40 to 60 percent saving over new parts. Wrecking yard components also are a good selection and the saving may be 20 percent over a rebuilt.

Radiator: A rebuilt radiator, called a "recore" because the core (the finned main section) is replaced, is at least 30 percent less expensive than a new radiator. If a shop refuses to install anything but a new radiator, take the car to a radiator specialist (most will deal with the retail customer). An even less expensive choice, if you can get the shop to install it, is a radiator from a wrecking yard (not all radiators are damaged when a car is wrecked).

Engine and Transmission: Brand-new engines and transmissions are virtually unobtainable except for current-model-year cars, so the choice is either a rebuilt or a used unit from a wrecking yard. Quality rebuilts are not cheap, so unless you plan to keep the car for two years or more, it is normally worthwhile to take a chance on a wrecking yard component. Reputable wreckers make basic checks of the used units they sell, so you're not gambling recklessly. The price difference between rebuilt and used engines is as much as $400, for a manual transmission $50 to $75, and for an automatic up to $125. Note: some manual and automatic transmissions cost very little to overhaul, so unless you are planning to sell the car within the year, the saving of less than $50 on a manual or $75 on an automatic would not be worthwhile.

Air Conditioning Compressor: A rebuilt is about 40 percent less costly than a new unit, and if the shop you go to refuses to install one, you should be able to find another that will.

Tires: *Retreaded tires* produced by a reputable firm carry the same guarantee as new tires, and they're about 40 to 50 percent cheaper. An equally good choice is a low-mileage used tire from a wrecking yard (it's about one-sixth the price of a new tire and as much as 80 to 90 percent of its life remains).

Batteries: If you plan to dispose of your car within a year, why spend up to $50 for a battery? A high-capacity used battery from a wrecking yard costs $7 to $10, and because wrecking yards only sell batteries from one- or two-year-old wrecks (or obviously new replacement batteries), you are reasonably sure of all the remaining battery life you need.

GUARANTEES

Every shop should guarantee the work it does. In many cases the extent of the guarantee is printed on the work order. If it is not, ask the man who takes your order, for the guarantee may vary according to the type of job.

On most repairs, the guarantee should be for 30 days or 1000 miles, whichever comes first. Major components, such as rebuilt transmissions and engines, should be guaranteed for at least 4000 miles or three months, and preferably for 6000 miles and six months. The guarantee should be 100 percent for both parts and labor, although some shops will guarantee the parts 100 percent and the labor 50 percent.

The "50-50" guarantee, in which the shop promises to do the job over if necessary for half the price of parts and labor, is not worth much. The shop usually can return any defective parts for full credit from the parts supplier, so it will get a good price for redoing the work when it adds the parts credit to the discounted labor bill. Clearly, a parts failure is normally not the shop's fault—but it isn't yours either.

Wrecking yard parts, of course, are not guaranteed at all by the shop that installs them, but if they fail in a short time, usually a week or two, the reputable wrecker will exchange them. You will still have to pay the mechanic's labor all over again, but for those situations in which the wrecking yard part is a good risk, take the chance and you'll be way ahead in the long run.

ROAD TESTS

If a problem only occurs in a certain driving situation, you may save a lot of money by asking that a mechanic or the service manager accompany you on a road test. That way you can point out exactly what you mean. Although many shops don't want to take the time to go for a ride with you, they also don't want to tie up a mechanic on a hunting expedition. The mechanic's search for the cause of an unclear problem is costly to you and it's not particularly profitable for a busy shop either.

Additionally, the last thing you or the shop wants is an argument over final results. Any poor ride or steering complaint, any noise or rattle that you want eliminated, and any special engine or transmission disorder rates a road test. Stories about the mechanic fixing the wrong rattles are legion—and the arguments with the customers that followed are unprintable.

A small charge may be made to cover the road test time, but it's usually worth paying if the road test is made with a service manager or mechanic. The dealerships and other shops that rely on their service salesmen to take care of road tests don't usually charge for this service, but such tests are of questionable value, for the typical service salesman is short on technical know-how and troubleshooting ability. This is another good reason to avoid car dealers when the car is not under warranty coverage.

| # Maintenance You Can Do

Doing some of the routine maintenance on a car accomplishes three important objectives in automobile ownership:

1. It makes sure the work gets done right.
2. It saves money.
3. It improves your understanding of the car for those jobs that require professional service.

The maintenance work in this section has been chosen for its suitability for beginners. Very few tools are necessary for this list of relatively straightforward jobs. A recent study showed more than fifty common repairs and maintenance tasks that an interested weekend mechanic could competently perform, so if you find that you enjoy weekend mechanicking, you'll find books that will help you expand your repertoire.

Very few jobs on a car require extraordinary physical strength. Although car repair is considered a man's field, there are hundreds of women in it too. The ones we've met have no special physical attributes (one was 4"-11" and weighed 97 pounds) and they do good work.

TOOLS

There's an old tradesman's axiom that goes, "Don't use force; get a bigger hammer." If you know the techniques and use the right tools, you'll always have the "bigger hammer" for the job.

The work you do on your own car will be of consistently high quality because you will not rush to take the shortcuts that many alleged professionals do. Parts that should be cleaned and tightened will be clean and tight when you're done.

You'll save money two ways: you'll have no labor charge, and you'll get the parts for less.

There are many discount houses, department stores, and retail auto parts stores that sell parts to car owners at substantially less than the list price you would pay in a professional shop.

Sears has been catering to do-it-yourself car owners for many years, selling tools and parts of generally good quality for prices that are measurably lower than repair shops' list prices, but not the lowest available. When Sears has a sale, however, its prices are very competitive, and if you don't have another source nearby, you can't go far wrong at Sears.

To find the best sources for parts and tools, check the automotive departments of the stores you patronize. Note the brands carried and compare prices. You should be able to get parts at 25 to 60 percent off the list price you would pay at professional shops. Inspect any tools you are considering very carefully, for you want them to last, even though you do not expect to give them everyday punishment.

If you own a foreign car, you probably will need metric wrenches (English cars are usually an exception: most use American-size nuts and bolts).

Here are some general guidelines to buying tools.

1. Screwdrivers: Get an assortment of good quality, for a cheap screwdriver will fail the first time you use it. "Vaco" is a good quality line we've seen in discount houses. Sears' also are excellent.

2. Hand wrenches: There are two basic types, "box" and "open-end," and some sets combine both types. The most popular American sizes are (in inches) 3/8, 7/16, 1/2, 9/16, 5/8, 11/16, 3/4, and 7/8. The most

popular metric sizes are (in millimeters) 6, 8, 9, 10, 11, 12, 13, 14, 17, and 19. For the jobs in this section, you need just one of these (for the oil drain plug) and a one-inch adjustable crescent wrench, *See Fig. 1.*

3. Socket wrenches: A socket is a cylindrical wrench that fits over a nut or bolt, *See Fig. 1.* It has a square hole in the top into which a ratchet can be fitted. This is a tool with a swivel mechanism that holds one way and free-wheels the other, with the directions changed for tightening or releasing by turning a knob. For work in tight quarters, you can obtain extension rods of various lengths and swivel joints (called universals) to fit between the ratchet and socket. The only job in this section that requires a ratchet and socket is spark plug replacement and you don't need a complete set, just a 3/8- or 1/2-inch drive ratchet (the 3/8 or 1/2 is the size of the square hole in the top of the socket and the ratchet projection into which it fits) and a 13/16-inch socket made for spark plug removal.

If you plan to expand your repertoire, you can buy a complete set of sockets with a ratchet and extension rod or two, using the size listings for hand wrenches as a guide. We recommend the 1/2-inch drive socket set, though sometimes a 3/8-inch drive set, which is trimmer, is required in tight spots. For a single problem, however, we suggest you buy just the one 3/8-inch drive socket and extension rod you need, plus an inexpensive adapter that permits it to be used with a 1/2-inch drive ratchet.

4. Pliers: The tool industry makes pliers in a thousand varieties. For the jobs in this section, an ordinary pair of slip-joint pliers is all you'll need. If you progress to other work, you may wish to buy needlenose pliers (which fit into tight places) and vise-type pliers (which can be locked on).

5. Jacks: The jack that comes with most cars is not only unsuitable for holding the car up while you work

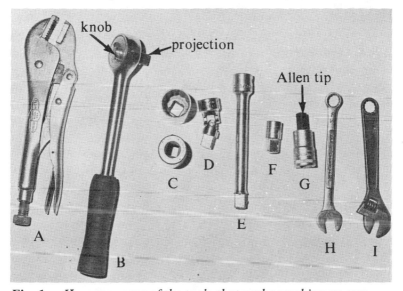

Fig. 1. *Here are some of the tools that make working on cars easier. From left to right:* "*A.*" *Vise-type pliers that can be locked at any setting.* "*B.*" *A ratchet—turning the knob one way sets the wrench for removing nuts or bolts, turning it the other way sets wrench for tightening them.* "*C.*" *Two sockets—upper one is upside down for an inside look. The socket's many inside ridges hold nut or bolt firmly for removal. The square hole in the top (see lower socket) accepts the square projection from the ratchet or one of the special adapters.* "*D.*" *Universal joint—note the square projection at the bottom end which fits into the socket; square hole (not visible) in the top end fits onto the ratchet.* "*E.*" *Extention rod, which permits positioning the ratchet away from the socket for convenience. The top end has a square hole (not visible) that fits over the ratchet projection and a square projection to fit into the socket.* "*F.*" *Adapter. This one has a 3/8-inch square hole in the top (not visible) and a ½-inch projection, to permit using a socket with a ½-inch square hole on a ratchet with a 3/8-inch projection.* "*G.*" *Socket with Allen-wrench tip. An Allen wrench is a male hex-head that fits into a special bolt with a female hex cut into the head.* "*H.*" *Combination open-end box wrench, the open-end at the bottom and the box at the top. The box is more convenient to use, but there are times only the open-end can fit into a tight place.* "*I.*" *Adjustable crescent wrench—an open-end wrench with an adjustable jaw so it can handle many sizes of bolts. It is larger than the single-size open-end to its left, so it may not fit into tight places.*

underneath it, it isn't even very safe for changing a wheel. We recommend a scissors jack and safety stands, *See Fig. 6,* particularly if you must (as is necessary on most cars) raise the car off the ground for such work as changing the engine oil and filter.

Before you can do any job under the hood of the car, you must be able to raise the hood. Every car has the hood release lever in a different spot, and you'll have to find the location and get the release procedure for your car from the owner's manual. If you plan to use your car's jack, you will also have to get the procedure from the owner's manual—again every manufacturer has a somewhat different model, and even the positioning of the jack varies from one year to the next.

UNDERHOOD CHECK OF FLUID LEVELS

Checking underhood fluid levels yourself may seem like a waste of time. After all, doesn't the service station attendant do it for you? The answer is that fewer stations than ever before do a complete check, the radiator water must be checked with the engine cold and, finally, if you do the checking yourself you can save some money.

ENGINE OIL

The most important check is the engine oil level. The location of the dipstick, *See Fig. 2,* you can learn from your owner's manual. There is a simple procedure, but it must be followed exactly:

1. Make sure the car is on reasonably level ground.
2. The engine must be shut off for at least three minutes to allow the oil to drain into the oil pan.
3. Pull the dipstick and wipe it off with a cloth or tissue.
4. Reinsert the stick, being careful to seat it, then pull and inspect, *See Fig. 3.*

dipstick
handle

Fig. 2. *You may have to look around for the engine oil dipstick, but it will always have a handle and will fit into a tube leading into the engine.*

Fig. 3. *Once you have the dipstick out, look at the markings— these indicate whether the engine has the proper amount of oil or needs an addition.*

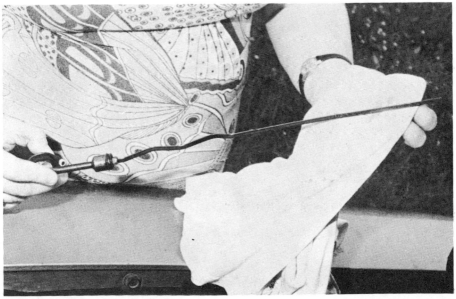

Only add oil when the dipstick shows the engine a quart low, for excess oil will be splashed past the piston rings or picked up by the Positive Crankcase Ventilation system and be deposited in the combustion chamber. In either case, it will be burned.

The oil is poured into the engine through the fill neck, which is covered by a twist-off or pull-off cap, *See Fig. 4.* The cap is usually on the valve cover. Note: special can-puncturing spouts are available at low cost for pouring oil into the engine.

Buy your oil in quantity at discount houses, limiting your purchases to such independent name brands as "Wolf's Head," "Pennzoil," "Castrol," "Kendall," "Quaker State," and "Valvoline" and, if available, gas station brands. Sears oil is also a quality product. Buying oil by the case may save you 60 cents per quart over service station prices. Buy a 10W-40 oil for year-round use, or a 30 weight for warm weather and a 20-20W for cold. A 5W-30 is recommended for very cold weather. Only purchase an oil that is recom-

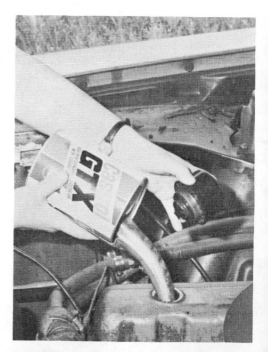

Fig. 4. *If the engine needs oil, remove the oil fill cap and pour in a quart. The special puncturing spout makes it easy. Both the oil fill cap and the Positive Crankcase Ventilation valve, which may resemble it, are in the valve cover. To distinguish between the two, look for a rubber ring, around the part—if you see it, that's the Positive Crankcase Ventilation valve, not the oil fill cap.*

mended for service "SD" or "SE" (these letters may be in fine print, but they should be somewhere on the can), for other oils may not provide the engine adequate protection. All oils are not the same.

AUTOMATIC TRANSMISSION OIL

The automatic transmission oil level is an extremely important check, for the most common cause of transmission malfunction and short life is low oil level. As with the engine, you may have to check your owner's manual to locate the dipstick, but in all cars currently in production, it projects into the rear of the engine compartment (from the transmission behind it), *See Fig. 5.*

Few service stations regularly check the transmission

Fig. 5. *Finding the automatic transmission dipstick may be difficult, but it usually projects from the rear of the engine compartment, whereas the engine oil dipstick will be closer to the front of the engine. If the transmission needs oil, it must be added through the dipstick tube, using a funnel and possibly a hose.*

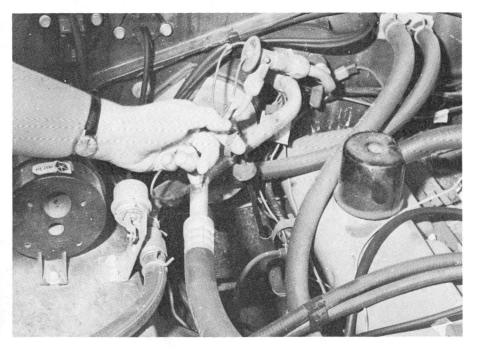

oil level, for it must be done with the engine running and the first thing the attendant asks you to do is to turn off the engine so he can safely pump the gas.

To make the check, run the car for at least 15 minutes, then let it idle. With the parking brake set and your foot on the brake pedal, move the gearshift lever from Park into each position for an instant, going all the way to Low, and then start back again. On Chrysler Corporation cars (Plymouth, Dodge, Chrysler, Imperial) and American Motors cars (Gremlin, Hornet, Matador, Javelin, Ambassador), stop in Neutral. On Ford (Ford, Lincoln, Mercury) and General Motors cars (Chevrolet, Buick, Oldsmobile, Pontiac, Cadillac), go all the way back to Park.

Pull the dipstick, wipe it off and reinsert it carefully. Many automatic transmission dipsticks require twisting to seat fully. Then remove the stick and inspect.

If the marking indicates that the transmission oil is a pint low, put in a pint. Unfortunately, transmission oil (also called fluid) comes only in quart cans, so you'll have to put the remainder in a jar. Under no circumstances should you wait until the transmission is a full quart low, and you should never overfill.

Be sure to buy the right kind of fluid. All Chrysler, General Motors and American Motors cars use "Dexron"-type fluid. Ford cars use "Type F" fluid. Transmission oil is added through the dipstick tube, so you'll need a narrow tip funnel.

Note: automatic transmissions should not lose very much oil, so a noticeably low level should make you suspicious. Check the ground under the transmission for oil leaks.

RADIATOR WATER

When the engine is cold, check the water level in the radiator (on cars with a partly transparent plastic expansion tank, you need not remove the cap). If the cap must be removed, press down on it with the heel of your hand and simultaneously twist counterclockwise until it comes to a stop.

Release the downward pressure and just twist the cap to a second stop, at which it can be lifted up. Some cars have caps with a lever in the top. With this design, lift the lever, then just twist the cap to a stop and lift it off.

The water level should be within a half inch of the bottom of the radiator cap neck on cars without expansion tanks. On cars with these tanks, check the manufacturer's recommendation in the owner's manual.

If the water level is low, add a mixture of water and anti-freeze (half of each), for the cooling system needs at least 50 percent anti-freeze all year round. If you just add water, you will dilute the mixture. Buy the anti-freeze at a discount house or supermarket and premix it in a jar yourself. You'll save about 60 cents per gallon.

BATTERY WATER

Most batteries have twist-off water caps on top, but some have a single cover for all the holes that you just lift off. Unless the water in your area is unusually hard, ordinary tap water can be added. If hard water is a problem, you probably have distilled water for your steam iron, and that is suitable for use in the battery.

The water in each hole should cover the vertical plates you can see and it can be as high as to the bottom of the hole.

WINDSHIELD WASHER

The windshield washer reservoir should be filled with a mixture of water and a windshield cleaner, and in the winter with a cleaner that contains anti-freeze. Some products are premixed with water, others are not, so check the container. If you buy the cleaner at a discount house, you can save at least 60 percent.

JACKING A CAR

If you insist on using your car jack, you'll have to rely on the instructions in the owner's manual. If you take our advice, you'll buy a scissors-type jack and a pair of safety stands. The jack and stands should be rated for at least 5000 pounds.

The operation of the scissors jack and stands should be obvious, but where to position them is not, so here's the information you need.

If you are just changing one wheel (as for a flat tire replacement), place the jack under the lower control arm in front or under the spring shackle in back, *See Fig. 6 and 7.*

Fig. 6. *Jacking the front of the car can be done with a scissors jack under the front crossmember. The long rod projecting forward from the jack is the handle, which is turned to raise or lower the jack. The jack was placed on a block so that it would raise the front of the car quite high, but this normally isn't necessary. The safety stands are under the lower control arms at each side. If you want to jack up only one front wheel, you may place the jack itself under the control arm; you'll find it easier to raise that wheel off the ground than to jack up the entire front end.*

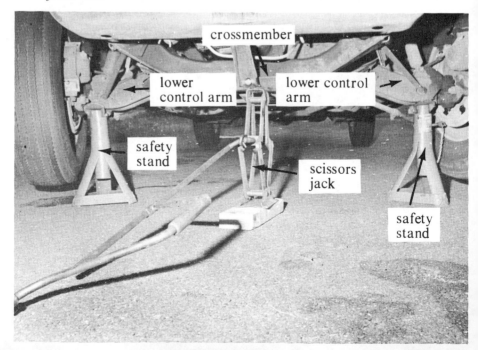

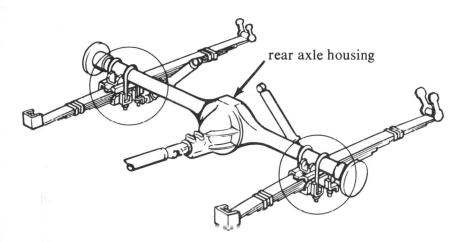

Fig. 7. *The rear end of the car can be jacked from under either spring shackle (the section in a circle), or if both wheels are to be raised, at the center from under the rear axle housing.*

If you are changing two front or two rear tires (as you might when installing snow tires already mounted on wheels), place the jack in the center under the rear axle housing *(Fig. 7)* in back or the crossmember in front (the crossmember is a thick steel rectangular piece that is bolted or welded from left to right sides of the underbody).

Before positioning yourself underneath the car for any work, set up the safety stands. In the rear they can be placed under a spring shackle or, if there is a solid tube from the rear axle housing to each wheel (as there is on almost all cars except Volkswagen), anywhere under the solid tube. In the front, they can be placed under the lower control arms or the crossmember at each side. Once the safety stands are in place and adjusted as high as possible, gradually lower the jack so that the car is resting on the stands, then leave the jack in place as extra protection. Try, with reasonable force, to jostle the car off the stands. If the car is going to fall off, it should happen when you're not underneath.

CHANGING A TIRE

Changing a tire is a partial misnomer, for what you're actually doing is changing a wheel with a tire on it. Removing a tire from the wheel requires special equipment.

Begin by prying off the wheel cover or hubcap. Use a large screwdriver and pry gradually all around. This is particularly important with a wheel cover, as you want to minimize damage to the tangs that hold the cover in place.

With the wrench provided with the car jack, slacken all the bolts on the wheel. If they're very tight, get a piece of pipe and put it partly over the end of the wrench to effectively lengthen the handle for better leverage, *See Fig. 8.* If they are extremely tight and appear to be rusty, spray penetrating oil solvent so that it will seep onto the threads. Wait a few minutes and try again.

Once the nuts or bolts are all loose, jack up the car until the wheel is two to three inches off the ground. Remove the nuts or bolts and take off the wheel.

Take the replacement wheel and line it up opposite the hub onto which it will be bolted and visually check the holes to be sure that the wheel will go right on. Turn the wheel until the lineup is right. Most wheels go on only one or two ways, and it isn't easy to hold a wheel off the ground and try to turn it until the holes line up.

Those cars that hold the wheels on with bolts rather than nuts usually have a couple of guides projecting from the hub to hold the wheel in place while you thread in the bolts.

Thread in all nuts or bolts finger tight. Note: nuts are always installed with the rounded edges against the wheel.

Lightly tighten all the nuts or bolts with the wrench, then lower the car to the ground and do the final tightening with the wrench. If you just use the wrench furnished with the car, it will be virtually impossible to overtighten even if you use all your strength.

Putting the hubcap or wheel cover back on may take real patience. Hubcaps are a bit easier. In most cases, they are whacked on over some dimples in the wheel. The tech-

Fig. 8. *If a wheel nut or bolt is very tight and the jack handle doesn't give sufficient leverage, put a piece of pipe over the end.*

nique is to fit the hubcap over all but one dimple, then with the heel of one hand, whack the cap at the final dimple while firmly holding the cap in place with your other hand.

Getting on a wheel cover is similar, except that while you're whacking at the end that's not in place, one of the sections that is in place may pop out. A rubber-faced hammer is better than the heel of your hand, which may take a beating after several unsuccessful attempts. There is no sure-fire procedure, but slightly bending in all the tangs may make things easier. Don't bend them in more than just a touch, or the cover will be loose.

REPLACING AN AIR FILTER

The air filter housing contains a filter element that should be inspected and replaced if necessary once every

Fig. 9. *Replacing an air filter element is very easy on most cars. Just undo the wingnut in the center of the air cleaner housing. You may need a pair of pliers if it's very tight, but no more. Lift off the cover and pull out the old element, which on almost all cars is made of pleated paper. If the exterior is dirty, install a new element.*

15,000 miles. In virtually all American cars today, the filter is a circular pleated-paper unit that is simplicity itself to change.

Remove the air filter housing top, a cover held on by a wingnut or some spring clips. The filter element can be lifted out and a new one dropped in, *See Fig. 9.* The cover then goes back on and the job is done.

Your engine needs a new element only if the old one is dirty. If it isn't, just rap it gently on the ground to knock off any loose dirt from the exterior circumference and reinstall it.

A dirty element should be discarded, but don't throw it away until you can compare it with the replacement you buy to make sure you've got the right part. In checking catalog listings for the filter element number, you will probably need to know no more than the number of cylinders and the number of carburetor barrels. If cubic inch displacement is required and you don't know it, the old filter element will help you make the correct choice from among the possibilities.

Most filters go in with either side up, but some do not. Look for the word "Top" embossed on one side of the filter, and if you don't see it, the side up doesn't matter.

Virtually all Volkswagens prior to this writing and a few Chevrolet models over the last several years have not had replaceable paper element filters. Instead they have filters that can be cleaned.

The job of cleaning is messy and not too successful even in professional shops. Many auto accessory stores carry pleated paper filters that replace these original equipment filters. If you wish to try cleaning the filters, however, here's how:

Chevrolet type: When you take off the air cleaner housing cover, you'll see a piece of polyurethane foam around a metal cage. That foam is the filter, and you must gently peel it off the cage without tearing it. Soak it in a pan of solvent (such as Gumout gasoline additive), gently squeeze it out and then allow it to air-dry. Then soak the element in a pan of clean engine oil, gently squeeze it out and reinstall on the cage.

Volkswagen type: The job really should be done with the complete air cleaner housing off the car, and removing it isn't difficult. Slacken the clamp at the bottom of the housing, disconnect a hose or two from the assembly and lift up and off. Newer models have both the clamp and a bracket that is mounted to the carburetor just below the clamp. Loosen the clamp, then undo the nut that holds the bracket with an adjustable crescent wrench. Pull the bracket from the threaded stud, disconnect the two hoses at the air cleaner and lift the housing up and off.

Undo the wingnut that holds the top of the filter, then lift it out. Look inside the housing and you'll see a small amount of oil. Dump this oil out and clean the inside of the housing with a rag soaked in solvent. Wipe the inside of the housing or allow it to air-dry.

The top part of the air cleaner holds the filter element, which is made of wire mesh. Dunk it in a pail of solvent and slosh it around for a few minutes. Remove from the solvent, shake out any solvent trapped inside and allow an hour to air-dry.

Put fresh engine oil in the lower part of the housing up to the mark. Fit the top half and reinstall on the engine.

CHANGING AN EXTERIOR LAMP

HEADLAMP

Most headlamps are held in by three little screws that are accessible after removing a decorative chrome or aluminum molding—also held by screws—that surrounds the lens, *See Fig. 10.* On a few cars, the entire grille must be removed, but in these cases the grilles are held on by only six to eight screws.

Once the molding or grille is off, take a few seconds to inspect the screws around the headlamp, for some of them control the aim of the lamp and must not be disturbed. You can identify the aim adjusting screws by the fact that they have little springs on them, whereas the ones that retain the headlamps thread through a metal retainer to a metal backing.

Most headlamp retainers are held by Phillips-head screws (the ones with the cross cut into the head) and you must use exactly the right size Phillips-head screwdriver. Too large a screwdriver won't fit in all the way and too small a screwdriver will not give a tight fit. In either case, you could ruin the cross cut in the head if you try to turn the

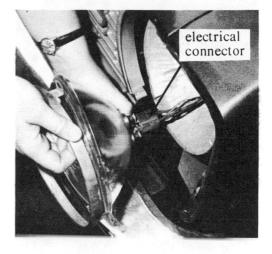

Fig. 10. *Most headlamps are covered by a decorative molding held on by screws. Remove this molding to begin replacement of a burned-out headlamp.*

electrical connector

screwdriver, and this will make it impossible to take out the screw by normal means.

Once you get the screws out, lift out the headlamp and retainer, and just pull off the electrical connector plug in the back of the headlamp, *See Fig. 11.* Push it onto the new headlamp (you can't do it wrong), and then reverse your removal procedure to finish the job.

Note: be sure you buy the right replacement headlamp. Cars with four headlamps use a different model than those with two lamps, and the high beam lamp is different from the low beam one in the four-eye system.

Fig. 11. *After removing the screws that hold the headlamp to the body (by means of a sheet metal retainer), undo the electrical connector from the lamp—it is just pulled off.*

On most cars the rear lamps are accessible through the trunk compartment. Look for a socket assembly (there'll be a wire going to it) and inspect it. Most sockets just come out with a gentle pull; a few must be twisted.

Removal of the bulb takes some care: Gently push down and twist (the bulb can be twisted only one way without force). You'll soon feel the bulb "want" to come up, so release the downward pressure and let it.

You must get an exact replacement for the bulb, both with respect to the number of filaments (stoplight-taillight bulbs have two, direction and side-marker bulbs have one) and the location of the locking tangs that project from the side, *See Fig. 12.* The bulb number on the side provides a positive check.

Fig. 12.   *This rear lamp has two filaments and so must its replacement. There was plenty of finger-gripping room on this bulb, but there may not be on your car. Here the lens was held on by external screws, but on most cars they are not, and the bulbs are accessible through the trunk compartment.*

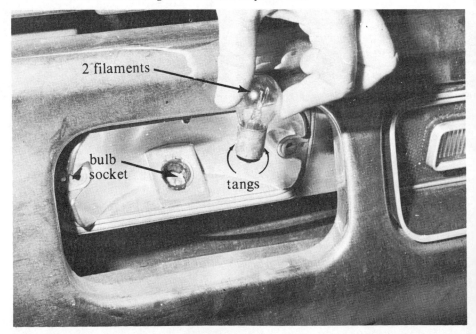

The front lamp bulbs are usually accessible after removing a lens held on by two to four screws. However, if you can't find the screws, leave the job to a service station. Some lamps require the removal of several parts, so you might as well let a professional shop struggle.

Even those that are behind a lens held on by easy-to-remove screws may pose a problem, for the bulb often doesn't project far enough out to get a good grip on it. If this is the case, don't take a chance without a special little tool that doesn't cost much but turns the job into a snap. It's a handle with a rubber cup that fits onto the bulb and holds it. You press down on the handle gently, twist and lift out the bulb. The tool, available at many retail auto supply stores, can also be used to install the new bulb.

As with rear lamps, make sure you've got the correct replacement bulb.

BATTERY SERVICE

There's a lot more to keeping a battery healthy than topping up the water level as described in "Underhood Check of Fluid Levels," (see page 139).

At least twice a year, you should give the battery a good exterior cleaning—not for appearance's sake, but to make sure that the battery stays charged and delivers the current. The primary cause of starting troubles, according to the American Automobile Association, is battery failure.

Corroded or loose battery cable terminals are probably responsible for most battery problems, and all you normally need to service them are an adjustable crescent wrench, a stiff wire brush and possibly a hammer.

With the wrench, slacken the nut that holds each cable terminal and twist the terminal on the battery post to loosen it, *See Fig. 13.* Then lift off. If the terminal is extremely tight, tap it back and forth with a hammer until it loosens, then twist it back and forth while lifting on.

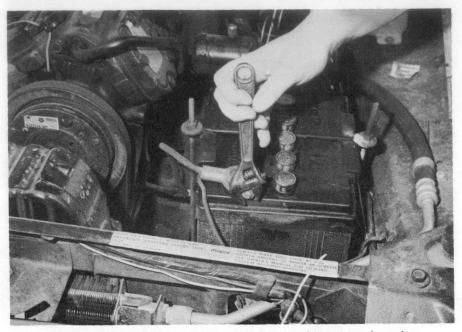

Fig. 13. *Slackening the nut on the battery cable terminal can be done with an adjustable crescent wrench.*

If you have an older car with spring-clip terminals, squeeze the tangs together with pliers while holding the other end of the terminal, *See Fig. 14.* With pliers and hand, twist back and forth while lifting up. If this type of terminal is loose when you're not squeezing the tangs, it must be replaced.

Before cleaning, inspect the cable terminal carefully. If it's rotted by the greenish-white corrosion that emanates from the battery, you should replace the terminal. The job requires a razor blade, a hacksaw and the adjustable crescent wrench.

Saw off the terminal at a point on the cable where the plastic insulation cover is good (there's enough slack in battery cables so you can remove at least an inch of cable and still have enough to reach the battery top), *See Fig. 15.* With the razor blade, cut away an inch of insulation covering to expose the wire. Install a replacement terminal, available in

150

Fig. 14. *If your car is an older one with this type of spring-clip terminal, squeeze the tangs with pliers and twist up and off.*

Fig. 15. *A very corroded terminal should be replaced. Just saw off the old one with a hacksaw, then cut off an inch of insulation from the end of the wire.*

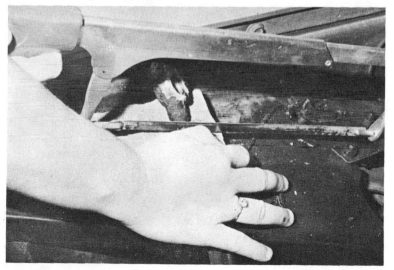

most auto supply stores and departments, as shown in *Fig. 16*. The replacement terminal is a two-piece device that clamps over the cable end *(Fig. 17)*; it can also be used to replace a spring-clip terminal that has become loose.

If the cable terminals are intact, but covered with any amount of greenish-white corrosion, they should be cleaned with a wire brush, *See Fig. 18*. Brush both the battery posts and the inside and outside surfaces of the cable terminal, then reinstall and tighten, *See Fig. 19*.

Fig. 16. *Insert the wire into the replacement terminal. If the cable has two wires, they both should be inserted.*

Fig. 17. *Put clamping cover over wires, insert bolts into holes and tighten down with the adjustable crescent wrench. This replacement terminal costs pennies and may save you the $20 a new cable replacement would cost at a garage.*

152

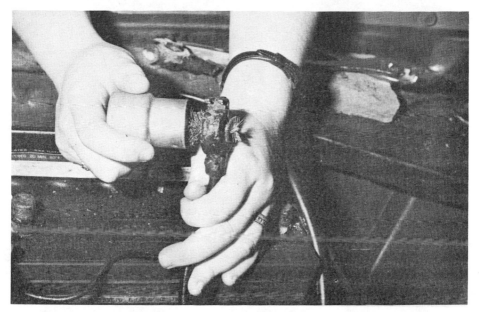

Fig. 18. *If the terminal is in reasonably sound shape, just clean it —inside and out—with a wire brush. The type shown is inexpensive and made for battery cables.*

Fig. 19. *Also clean the battery post with the wire brush. This type, which also does the job on battery cables, we bought for 39 cents.*

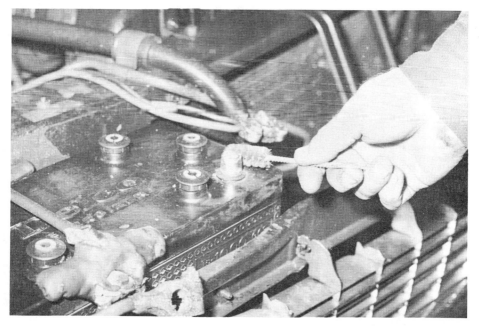

Now clean the top of the battery with a baking soda and water solution, and wipe dry. To retard corrosion, coat the battery terminals with a thin film of petroleum jelly.

If you regularly clean off corrosion, the battery hold-down will also stay in good condition. This bracket, which keeps the battery in place—preventing it from vibrating and cracking—may also get corroded on some cars. Wire-brush it clean and coat with an acid-resistant paint. Or, if it's really bad, replace it.

Even if the hold-down is in good shape, check it for tightness. If it doesn't completely keep the battery from moving, it's loose.

Note: batteries with cables that bolt into the side of the battery, like those used on late-model General Motors cars as original equipment, normally stay reasonably clean and free of corrosion and may not require any service other than a check of the plastic sleeve under the cable terminal retaining bolts (inspect it for electrical erosion and replace if damaged) and an occasional top cleaning.

If your car ever needs a replacement battery and you have the GM side-terminal type, you will find that a duplicate replacement is more expensive than a top-terminal one. You can buy the less expensive top-terminal design and have the shop selling you the battery install it with a conversion adapter. If you are buying a used battery from a wrecking yard and must adapt it yourself, you have two choices: obtain these special adapters from an auto supply store or saw off the side terminals and install the replacement top terminal described earlier. One caution: before you do any sawing, make sure there's enough slack in the cables so they will reach up to the top of the battery.

CHANGING ENGINE OIL AND FILTER

The engine oil and filter should be changed every 4000 miles or three months, whichever comes first. The job requires a wrench to remove the oil pan drain plug, an oil filter wrench and a pan into which to drain the engine oil.

If you are not planning to buy a complete set of wrenches, you can measure the oil pan drain plug and buy only the one you need. Almost any moderately flat pan will do as a drain pan so long as it holds five quarts of liquid. The oil filter wrench is perhaps $1.

Buy your filter from a discount house, and you'll save up to $4. Be sure you stick to a reputable brand, for like engine oil, all filters are not the same. The leading brands are: "AC," "Purolator," "Fram," "Motorcraft," "Walker," "Deluxe," "MoPar," "NAPA," "Atlas" and "Wix." Other acceptable brands are "Lee," "Baldwin," and "STP." In general, the only information you need to get the correct oil filter is the make of car and the number of engine cylinders.

The job requires working underneath, so you must determine whether or not you can reach the oil pan drain plug and oil filter without jacking up the car.

The first step is to find the drain plug and filter. Locate the engine from underneath the car, and then the sheet metal oil pan at the bottom. Somewhere at the bottom of that pan is the drain plug. It will appear to be a bolt that holds nothing, just threaded into the pan.

The filter should be easier to locate. On almost all cars (except most Volkswagens, which have no filter), it is a cylindrical spin-on unit with a sheet metal case. On most cars, it can be reached from the top of the engine compartment.

The drain plug is relatively tight, so you will need a wrench with a reasonably long shank to provide adequate leverage. To measure the size, just put a piece of typing paper over the hexagonal head of the plug and fold down on the paper carefully to form the outline of the plug's head. Remove the paper and measure the distance from one intersection of sides diagonally across to another. This width is the size of the wrench you'll need. If your car has metric-sized nuts and bolts, measure with a ruler calibrated in millimeters. Some foreign cars have Allen-type drain plugs. The Allen design simply means that the hexagonal is cut into the head of the bolt, and a special type of wrench is needed.

You'll have to get the wrench from a foreign car parts store.

If you must jack up the car to do an oil or filter change, remember our strong recommendation in "Jacking a Car" (see page 139)—use a scissors jack and safety stands. You will be jacking up the front of the car, so follow the instructions for front positioning. If you only need access from one side of the car, you can simply jack up that one side, placing the jack under the lower control arm.

The engine should be warm so that the oil drains as completely as possible.

Place the drain pan underneath where it can catch the oil and then get under yourself. Put the wrench on the plug and pull counterclockwise to loosen, *See Fig. 20.* Remember that you're working from underneath, and counterclockwise may seem like clockwise, so if the plug doesn't loosen with reasonable pressure, make sure you're properly oriented. If the plug is really stuck, tap the end of the wrench shank with a hammer to shock it loose.

Loosen but do not take the drain plug out with the wrench. Remove the wrench and now position the drain pan directly under the plug. Take the plug out the rest of the way by hand. As you get to the final thread on the plug, pull the plug away very quickly or you'll get a squirt of oil down your arm.

Allow several minutes for as much oil as possible to trickle out, then reinstall the drain plug by hand until it's finger tight. Give it a final tightening with the wrench.

How tight is tight enough? You might want a practice round or two. If you have to exert some force to loosen the plug, it is tight enough. If it takes virtually no effort, the plug is a bit too loose. Don't give it all your strength, for overtightening could ruin the plug's fit into the pan and cause an oil leak. The first time you change the oil yourself, recheck the plug for tightness periodically and watch for leaks. That way you can test yourself until you get the feel.

Next proceed to the oil filter. The standard oil filter wrench is a strap device that opens up if you move the han-

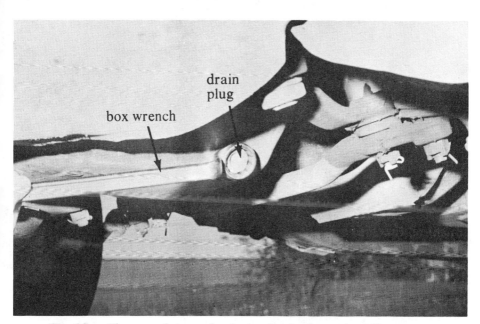

Fig. 20. *The wrench is on the drain plug in the engine oil pan. A long-handle wrench is necessary to give you the leverage to loosen the plug. Once you have the plug loose, place the drain pan underneath, unthread the plug by hand and pull away.*

dle one way and closes the other, *See Figs. 21 and 22.* The object is to install the wrench over the filter so that it closes up when you move the handle counterclockwise. In this way, it will grip the filter firmly as you turn counterclockwise to loosen the unit.

Position the wrench so there is swing room for the handle. A minute or two of test positioning should make this easy.

Use the wrench only to loosen the filter, completing the spin-off by hand. Make sure you hold the filter so the open end is up as you remove it, or you'll spill the oil inside it.

Take the new filter and smear some clean oil on the

Fig. 21. *Before you look for it on the engine, we thought you'd like to see what the engine oil filter is, and how the strap-type wrench fits on it for filter removal. The part of the filter you're seeing is the end that is against the engine.*

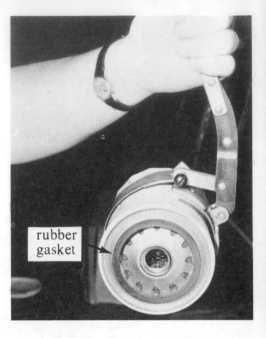

rubber gasket

Fig. 22. *Now you know why we showed you how things looked off the car. This on-the-car photo proves that the job can be done, even if some parts obscure the filter.*

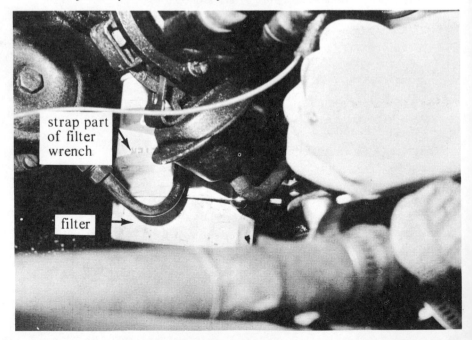

strap part of filter wrench

filter

rubber gasket on top of the open end. Thread on the new filter by hand, and then firmly hand-tighten it. When doing the hand tightening, be sure that the filter exterior and your hands are clean of oil, so there's no slippage, which would leave the filter loose. Never use the filter wrench to tighten the filter, for you'll surely overtighten it. Inasmuch as a filter may self-tighten a bit in use, as hand tight as you can make it is just fine.

Complete the job by pouring in the fresh supply of oil through the oil fill neck. We mention this only because many beginning weekend mechanics, in their enthusiasm over successfully draining the oil, refitting the drain plug and installing a new filter, forget this final step and cause some engine damage before they realize what they have done.

REPLACING SPARK PLUGS

Spark plugs should be replaced every 12,000 miles, and by doing the job yourself you can save about $5 on the parts alone. The job isn't hard, and usually requires only a spark plug gauge, ratchet and a 13/16-inch spark plug socket (this special socket, for foreign or American cars, is very deep and has a sponge rubber insert to hold the plug). In some cases, you will need an extension rod and possibly a universal joint.

Note: there are cars on which the spark plugs are not accessible from the top of the engine compartment, generally cars with V-8 engines, air conditioning and power steering. In fact, on some cars, the job of replacing plugs may require disconnecting the air conditioning compressor, power steering pump and perhaps even the generator. Don't try the job unless you can remove all the plugs without these major disconnections. The sensible procedure is to disconnect each spark plug wire and see if you can get your ratchet wrench setup on the spark plug and still be able to swing the handle.

Although you can do the job on most Volkswagens, they present a special problem. There are two spark plugs on each side, and they're covered by metal sheathing. The job must be done entirely by feel, but a ratchet, a very short extension and a socket are all you really need aside from a careful touch.

Here is an important tip on disconnecting spark plug wires at the plugs: never pull on the wire itself, or it will come apart internally, and the engine will misfire. Instead, grab at the rubber boot over the spark plug end, twist back and forth and pull straight out, *See Fig. 23*. A fair amount of tug may be necessary.

Treat each plug as a separate job—disconnect only one plug wire at a time and replace that plug before going on to the next. That way, you'll be sure to reconnect the wires correctly. If you switch wires, the engine will misfire.

Fig. 23. *This is the right way to remove the spark plug wire, with your fingers on the wire's rubber terminal.*

The 13/16-inch spark plug socket is a specially deep one, for it must fit onto the plug's hexagonal head, which is at the midpoint of the plug, *See Fig. 24.*

Set the ratchet so that it freewheels in the clockwise direction and holds in the counterclockwise one, then place the ratchet and socket assembly onto the spark plug, making sure that it fits onto the hex head. When it does, it will hold against counterclockwise pressure.

Fig. 24. *With the plug wire disconnected, this is what you'll see. The hexagonal surface that is in contact with the engine is what the deep spark plug socket engages.*

Put the heel of one hand against the top of the ratchet, or grasp the extension rod if you are using a universal joint, to brace the wrench setup on the spark plug's hex head, *See Fig. 25.* Freewheel the ratchet handle until it is in a position

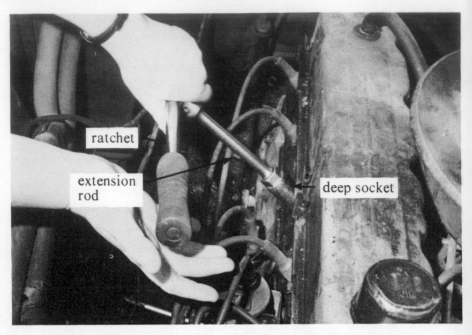

Fig. 25. *The spark plug socket is on the hexagonal surface, an extension rod is in the socket and the ratchet is in the extension rod. If the plug is tight, a whack with the heel of the hand on the ratchet handle should shock it loose.*

convenient for good leverage, then pull. Usually the plug will loosen and you can continue to use the ratchet until the plug is quite loose. Remove the wrench and do the final dethreading by hand. On Volkswagens, only disconnect the ratchet once you've loosened the plug and twirl the extension by hand, for you will not be able to reach in and get your fingers on the plugs unless you have very small hands.

If the plug is very tight and a reasonable amount of steady force on the handle doesn't loosen it, don't—as we recommended for removing wheels—get a piece of pipe to put over the handle for greater leverage. The odds are you'll cock the socket and break the spark plug, which may make its removal difficult. Instead, while holding the ratchet as described, use the heel of your free hand to whack the handle, which normally will shock the plug loose.

Your replacement plugs should be a reputable brand, such as "Champion," "AC," "Autolite," "Prestolite," "MoPar," "Atlas," "Lodge," "Marchal," "Bosch" or "Sears." They can be purchased in discount houses for up to 60 percent off the list price (in the case of "Sears" plugs, the selling price is about the same as for other brands at discount houses, for "Sears" plugs are not sold at normal trade outlets and do not have the higher list price of these brands).

It is most important that you get the right spark plugs. Discount house clerks normally do no more than give you a spark plug catalog, and you will have to pick out the part number. A typical listing will identify the car by year, model, number of cylinders and cubic inch displacement of the engine. If you don't have the necessary information, we suggest you remove one spark plug as explained, read the number on the ceramic exterior and look for an interchange chart in the catalog. All leading spark plug manufacturers list their equivalent of their competitors' product part numbers.

You must adjust the gap between the two electrodes with an inexpensive (about $1) special tool called a spark plug gauge, *See Fig. 26.* It has little pieces of wire of different thickness. You choose the correct one for your car and insert it between the electrodes.

It should go between them with some drag, which tells you that the gap equals the thickness of the wire gauge. If the gap is too large or too small, it must be adjusted by bending the side electrode. If the gap is too large, close it with one of the special prongs built into the gauge, *See Fig. 27.* If it is too small, bend it away with a small screwdriver between the electrodes. The first time around, it will take a few minutes to get each gap to conform to the car manufacturer's specifications, but you'll soon be able to gap all the plugs in five minutes or less.

Note: if the spark plug gap is not listed in the catalog, ask the store to check its ignition system specifications

Fig. 26. *Measuring the gap between two spark plug electrodes is done with this wire gauge. The wire of a thickness specified by the car manufacturer, should go between the electrodes with light drag.*

chart. If it doesn't have one, check your owner's manual, which may have a specifications section giving this information. The plug gap for virtually all American cars is 0.035 inch.

Thread in the new spark plug until it is finger tight. On Volkswagens, insert the plug into the sponge holder in the socket, fit the extension rod and use that as a handle. Don't try to force a plug in, particularly on a VW where you're working only by feel.

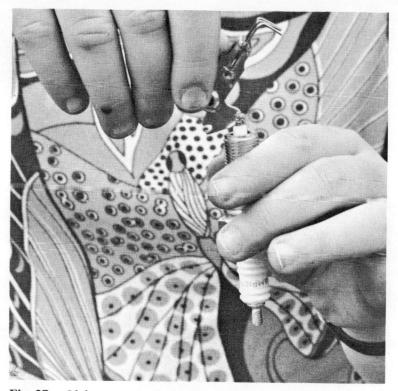

Fig. 27. *If the gap must be changed, bend the end of the side electrode with the gauge tool's special prongs.*

Once the plug is finger tight, put the wrench back on and tighten no more than an additional quarter turn if the plug is the type with a steel washer; one-sixteenth of a turn if it has no washer. All you want is to insure that the plug is tight enough to stay there. However, many people overtighten, which can make it extremely difficult to change the plug next time.

Now thread the little cap onto the top of the spark plug. Note: if the cap has different ends, check the old spark plug to see which end is up. Then push the plug wire on until it seats on the cap, *See Fig. 28.*

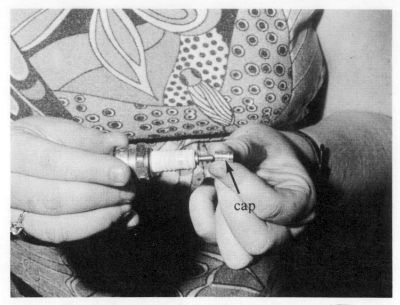

Fig. 28. *Once the plug is reinstalled, thread the cap at right onto the end of the plug and tighten with pliers. Note: some plugs come with the cap already on.*

THREADING IN A PART—EASY DOES IT

Threading in anything—nut, bolt, spark plug, filter or drain plug—can sometimes be frustrating. For some reason, the threads just won't catch properly.

Don't lose patience and don't try to force the part—if you do, you will surely cross the threads and ruin something. Take a coffee break and remember that the refusal of a part to be threaded in is something that happens to professional mechanics all the time.

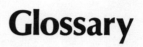

Glossary

A

AIR CLEANER—a sheet metal cannister on top of the carburetor air horn that removes dirt particles from the air before it goes into the air horn. The filtering is done by a part called a filter element, which is usually made of a special type of paper.

AIR CONDITIONING COMPRESSOR—a pump that draws refrigerant gas from the condenser, compresses it, and delivers it to the expansion valve as a liquid.

AIR CONDITIONING CONDENSER—a finned, tubular part that resembles a radiator and is positioned in front of it. In this part, the refrigerant gas gives up heat absorbed in the evaporator.

AIR COOLING—a system of engine cooling using a fan that blows air over various exterior sections of the engine. Generally, the exterior parts have fins to channel the air flow for maximum effectiveness. The Volkswagen is the best-known example of an air-cooled engine car.

AIR-FUEL CHARGE (also called AIR-FUEL MIXTURE)—a mixture of gasoline droplets and air in a ratio that can easily be burned in the combustion chamber of an engine; typically 12 to 14 parts of air (by volume) to one part of gasoline.

AIR HORN—the cylindrical portion of the carburetor, through which the air flows on its way into the engine. A tube from a fuel bowl projects into the air horn, and the air rushing by draws fuel droplets out of it to form the AIR-FUEL CHARGE. The air horn is also called a barrel, and engines may have one-, two- or four-barrel carburetors.

ALTERNATOR—a generator that produces alternating current. Since the car electrical system requires direct current, electronic components in the alternator called diodes are used to change the AC to DC.

ANTI-FREEZE—a chemical

mixed with the water in the engine cooling system to lower the freeze point in winter and raise the boiling point in summer. The cooling system should have at least 50 percent anti-freeze.

AXLE—the support assembly for two wheels. In the conventional car, the front axle is merely a support, and the rear axle contains a small gearbox called a differential, plus axle shafts, to transfer engine power to the wheels in addition to providing support. In the front-wheel-drive car, the rear axle is merely a support, while the front axle both supports and transfers power.

B

BALL BEARING—a bearing consisting of round steel balls in a circular holder.

BANDS—circular clamps of friction material used in the automatic transmission. When they are clamped on, they keep certain gears from turning, resulting in a change in the gear ratio in the transmission.

BATTERY—a device that stores electrical energy in chemical form.

BEARING—a smoothly finished support for a moving part. Rollers or round balls in cylindrical holders, which need only periodic applications of grease, are used where a fresh supply of lubricant cannot be pumped into the bearing. Plain cylindrical shells are used where lubricant can be pumped in—to support the engine crankshaft and camshaft, for example.

BELT—a layer of fabric or steel cord under the tread of a tire that serves to brace the tread. See also DRIVE BELT.

BRAKE DRUM—a cakepan-shaped part, against the inner sides of which are pushed semi-circular shaped brake shoes. The drum is bolted to the wheel, and when the friction force of the shoes stops it, the wheel also stops.

BRAKE LINING—the friction

material attached to the brake shoes.

BRAKE MASTER CYLINDER—a cylinder filled with special oil. When you step on the brake pedal, you actuate linkage that pushes a piston inside the cylinder against the oil, transmitting fluid under pressure through tubing to move the brake shoes.

BRAKE SHOES—pieces of steel to which asbestos friction material is bonded or riveted. When pushed against a drum or disc to which the wheel is bolted, they create a friction force that stops the wheel.

BRAKING SYSTEM—the components that react, when you step on the brake pedal, to apply friction to a drum or disc bolted to each wheel; this friction brings the part, and the wheel bolted to it, to a stop.

BREAKER (IGNITION) POINTS—a pair of round contacts in the distributor. They form a switch that is closed when they touch, open when one contact is pushed away from the other. The movement is directed by a cam on a shaft in the distributor. The opening of the points is the signal that creates a spark at the spark plugs, firing the air-fuel mixture.

C

CALIPER—the C-shaped clamp mounted over the edge of the disc in a disc braking system. It uses a piston to push brake shoes against the faces of the disc to stop the wheel.

CALL LIMIT—the maximum amount you agree to pay for repair without being notified in advance of the work being done.

CAM—a specially shaped projection used in the automobile to push a spring-loaded part open against spring pressure. Examples: cams push on the valve linkage to open intake and exhaust valves, and against one of the ignition breaker points to open them.

CAMSHAFT—a rotating shaft that operates the engine's fuel, ignition, lubrication and valve systems, by means of gears and teardrop-shaped projections called cams. It has a gear at the front that is turned by a gear from the crankshaft, either by direct mesh or by a special chain, called the timing chain, wrapped around both of them.

CAMSHAFT JOURNAL—a mirror-smooth round section of the camshaft that is surrounded by close-fitting circular bearings which support the journals —and thus the camshaft of which they are part.

CARBURETOR—the device that mixes fuel from the fuel pump with clean air from the air filter to create a combustible mixture for the cylinders.

CENTRIFUGAL ADVANCE —a pair of half-moon-shaped weights attached to the distributor shaft. At high engine speed, they swing outward and reposition the upper half of the shaft so that the breaker points open earlier, automatically advancing the spark timing to adjust for the needs of the faster-running engine.

CHOKE—a plate on the top of the carburetor's air horn that restricts the air flow when the engine is cold, thus providing an air-fuel mixture that is richer with fuel than normal. As the engine warms up, the plate pivots to a vertical position at which it poses no restriction to air flow. Most cars today have automatic chokes which are thermostatically controlled. Some cars, primarily imported models, have manual chokes with the plates connected by linkage and/or cables to a knob on the dashboard.

CLUTCH—generally, a friction device that joins the engine to a standard transmission. But clutches are also used in automatic transmissions and in some types of differentials.

CLUTCH SLIPPAGE—failure of the clutch friction disc to hold firmly, permitting power to be lost. In a manual transmission car, the disc slippage is against the flywheel. In an automatic transmission, there are several friction discs and slippage refers to their failure to properly join parts for complete transfer of power. In either case, the sensation to the driver is that despite heavy foot pressure on the gas pedal, and an immediate speedup of the engine, the car doesn't move commensurately.

COIL—the part of the ignition system where the high-voltage electricity needed to fire the air-fuel mixture is created. The coil has two windings of wire, a thick winding through which low-voltage current is passed to create an electromagnet and a thin winding. When the ignition breaker points are opened, a magnetic field created in the thick winding collapses on the thin winding, which sharply increases the current's voltage.

COMBUSTION CHAMBER —a cuplike recess in the cylinder head in which the air-fuel mixture is burned. Each chamber has an intake valve to admit the air-fuel mixture, an exhaust valve to allow burned gases to escape, and a spark plug to ignite the mixture.

COMPRESSION GAUGE—a pressure gauge that measures the effectiveness of the engine in compressing the air-fuel mixture in the combustion chamber.

COMPRESSION RATIO—a measure of the degree to which the air-fuel mixture is compressed. Actually, it measures the volume of the cylinder and combustion chamber with the piston in the low position compared to the volume with the piston at the top of the stroke. In a typical engine, the compression ratio is 9 to 1.

CONDENSER—an electrical shock absorber. When the coil creates the high voltage to fire the air-fuel mixture, the condenser temporarily absorbs stray voltage surges to prevent weakening of the spark and to prevent current from prematurely burning the ignition breaker points. Also see AIR CONDITIONING CONDENSER.

CONNECTING ROD—a rod connected to the piston at the upper end and the U-shaped section of the crankshaft at the lower end. It transfers downward force produced by combustion of the air-fuel mixture to the crankshaft.

CONNECTING ROD BEARING—a bearing between the lower end of the connecting rod and the crankshaft journal to which it is attached. It is made in two half-moon shells for ease of installation.

CONTROL ARM—a suspension part that connects the steering knuckle (and the wheel attached to it) to the car body. The typical front suspension has an upper and a lower control arm at each side, one connecting to the top of the knuckle, the other to the bottom, each connection made by a ball joint.

COOLING SYSTEM—the system that removes excess heat formed during combustion in the engine. In most engines WATER COOLING is used; in some, AIR COOLING.

CORE—a defective component that is being replaced in its entirety. The component may have to be exchanged, or the parts supplier levies an additional charge ("core charge") for the replacement part.

CRANKCASE—the part of the engine below the lower ends of the cylinders: the oil pan and the lower part of the engine block which houses the crankshaft.

CRANKSHAFT—a shaft with U-shaped sections to which the piston connecting rods are attached. The crankshaft converts the up-and-down motion of the pistons into rotary motion which it transfers to the transmission.

CRANKSHAFT JOURNAL —a mirror-smooth round section of the crankshaft that is surrounded by close-fitting circular bearings which provide support. Main bearing journals are the sections held to the

174

block by caps with bolts; connecting rod journals are the sections around which the lower ends of the connecting rods are bolted.

CRANKSHAFT MAIN BEARING—a bearing between the crankshaft journal and the engine block, into which it is bolted. The bearing is made in two half-moon shells for ease of installation.

CROSSMEMBER—a thick, steel rectangular section that braces the chassis.

CUBIC-INCH DISPLACEMENT—the total volume of all the cylinders as measured with the pistons at the bottom of their strokes.

CYLINDER—a hole bored in the engine block, into which is fitted a movable plug called a piston. The typical engine has four, six or eight cylinders.

CYLINDER HEAD—the top of the engine, cast into the underside of which are the combustion chambers. When bolted onto the block, it covers the cylinders and provides the enclo-sures (cylinder and combustion chamber) in which combustion of the air-fuel mixture takes place. In all modern engines, the valves are also in the head, a design called "overhead valve."

CYLINDER HEAD GASKET —a thin sheet, generally a sandwich of steel and asbestos, placed between the cylinder head and the top of the engine block to prevent leakage of fluids and the compressed air-fuel mixture at the joint.

D

DIFFERENTIAL—a set of gears in the center of the rear axle assembly which change the direction of the power transmitted by the driveshaft, and also allow one rear wheel to turn faster than the other when the car is turning.

DIPSTICK—a flat steel rod used to measure the oil level in the engine, automatic transmission or power steering reservoir.

DISC BRAKES—a braking system in which a caliper clamps friction-material-coated parts called brake shoes against the inner and outer faces of a disc bolted to the wheel.

DISTRIBUTOR—the component driven by a gear on the camshaft that distributes sparks to the spark plug wires.

DISTRIBUTOR CAM—the part of the distributor shaft on which there are projections that push open the ignition breaker points according to a built-in schedule.

DISTRIBUTOR CAP —the plastic cap on top of the distributor into which the spark plug wires and a wire from the coil are inserted.

DISTRIBUTOR SHAFT—the rotating shaft inside the distributor. It has a cam that opens the ignition breaker points, and a rotor on top that accepts the spark electricity from the coil and transfers it to the spark plug wires.

DRIVE BELT—a stiff rubber belt that transfers power from the crankshaft pulley to the pulleys of such accessory devices as the power steering, air conditioning, generator and water pump.

DRIVESHAFT—the long piece of piping that transfers power from the transmission to the rear axle assembly.

DRIVESHAFT UNIVERSAL JOINTS—swivel joints built into the driveshaft to allow its installation at an angle.

DRIVE TRAIN—all the parts that take power from the engine and transfer it to the wheels: the clutch or torque converter, transmission, driveshaft and rear axle assembly.

E

ELECTRONIC IGNITION— an ignition system that uses transistors to help create high-voltage electricity in the coil.

ENGINE BLOCK—the part of the engine that has the cylinders, pistons, crankshaft and, usually, the camshaft.

ENGINE MISFIRE—an irregularity in engine performance in which one or more cylinders fail to properly burn the air-fuel mixture.

ENGINE MOUNTS—metal-and-rubber sandwiches that hold the engine to the car chassis.

ENGINE OIL—a lubricant designed for use in a car engine. It is identified by thickness (5, 10, 20, 30, 40, 50) and by service recommendations (SC, SD, SE). Dual-thickness oils, such as 1OW-40, have different thickness ratings at different temperatures: a 1OW-40 has the thickness of a 10 weight oil at low temperatures and a 40 weight at high temperatures, making it suitable for year-round use. Letter ratings indicate oil's performance: an SE oil is recommended for all cars, an SD oil is suitable for 1970 and earlier cars only, and SC oil for 1967 and earlier cars.

EVAPORATOR—the part of the air conditioning system in the passenger compartment. It contains tubing into which refrigerant gas flows, absorbing heat from the surrounding air and cooling it. A fan blows this cooler air out of louvred vents.

EXHAUST MANIFOLD—the part of the system that carries the exhaust gases from the exhaust ports to the exhaust pipe.

EXHAUST PIPE—a pipe that takes the exhaust gases from the exhaust manifold to the sound-modifying parts—the resonators and mufflers.

EXHAUST PORTS—passages in the cylinder head that lead from the exhaust valve to the exhaust manifold, to channel the burned gases into the exhaust system.

EXHAUST SYSTEM—the system that carries the burned air-fuel mixture from the combustion chamber and expels it into the atmosphere: the exhaust manifold, exhaust pipe, and mufflers.

EXHAUST VALVE—the valve in the combustion

chamber that opens to allow burned fuel gases to flow into the exhaust system.

F

FLOODING—an engine stalling condition caused by an excessive amount of fuel flowing out of the carburetor fuel bowl into the air horn.

FLYWHEEL—the heavy round plate mounted on the rear of the crankshaft to help smooth out the rotary motion of the shaft. It has a gear pressed onto its outer circumference that meshes with the starter gear, so that when the starter turns, the flywheel also turns. Because the flywheel is bolted to the crankshaft, the crankshaft turns, setting in motion the events that will soon have it running on its own. Bolted to the back face of the flywheel is the manual clutch spring pressure plate or a part of the automatic transmission

torque converter.

FOUR-WHEEL DRIVE—a design in which power is transmitted from the engine to all four wheels instead of just two. The traction is considerably improved, but at great expense and complexity. Hence the design is used only on so-called off-road vehicles, such as Jeeps, and on special towing vehicles.

FRICTION DISC—a round plate coated with an asbestos friction material that is mounted on a shaft going into the transmission and is pressed against the back face of the flywheel by a spring pressure plate. Pressing down on the clutch pedal releases the spring pressure on the friction disc, allowing the transmission to be shifted into neutral and the engine to run while the car is stopped. Because the friction disc is the only part that joins the engine to the transmission, it must hold firmly against the flywheel (see CLUTCH SLIPPAGE). Friction discs are also used inside an automatic transmission to lock components together for shifting.

FRONT END—common term for the front suspension and steering linkage.

FRONT WHEEL BEARINGS —the bearings that support the front wheels and brake drum or disc on the steering knuckle. They are usually roller bearings, resembling many wheels of a roller skate mounted in a circular holder.

FRONT-WHEEL DRIVE—a design in which power from the engine is transmitted to the front wheels instead of the rear wheels. The front-wheel-drive design, by transmitting power to the wheels that can turn, provides better traction. Additional traction is provided by the fact that the weight of the engine is on the wheels being driven.

FUEL PUMP—a device that draws fuel from the gas tank and pumps it to the carburetor. On most cars this is a mechanical unit with an arm that is actuated by a cam on the camshaft. On some cars it is an electric unit, mounted some distance from the engine, which protects it from the heat of the engine, thus preventing a temporary pump malfunction called vapor lock.

FUEL SYSTEM—the group of components that deliver a mixture of air and gasoline to the engine: the gas tank, fuel pump, carburetor, and intake manifold. The fuel pump draws fuel from the tank, through tubing, and pumps it, through tubing, into the carburetor. Here it mixes with air and flows through the intake manifold into ports (passages) that go to the combustion chamber.

G

GASKET—a sheet of material placed between two flat surfaces that are bolted together to compensate for any irregularities in the surface. The gasket prevents fluid or air leaks at the joint.

GEAR—a circular part with teeth cut into the circumference. The teeth mesh with those of another gear to transfer power.

GEAR RATIO—the ratio of the number of teeth on one gear to the number on another with which it meshes. This gives the relative speeds of the gears: a gear with 36 teeth in mesh with one with 12 represents a 3 to 1 gear ratio, and the larger gear will turn at only one third the speed of the smaller one.

GENERATOR—a device driven by a belt from the crankshaft pulley to convert a small amount of engine power into electricity.

GOVERNOR—in an automatic transmission, the road-speed-sensitive device that sends a fluid pressure signal into the transmission to govern the speeds at which it will shift.

H

HEAT RISER—a thermo-statically controlled valve built into the exhaust manifold that directs exhaust gases when the engine is cold to heat the intake manifold for better fuel mixing with the air.

HYDRAULIC SYSTEM—the system of fluid-filled cylinders with pistons, plus interconnecting tubing, that transfers brake pedal movement into movement of brake shoes against drums or discs.

HYDRAULIC VALVE LIFTER—a valve lifter that uses engine oil to absorb shock and smooth out its operation.

I

IDENTIFICATION PLATE—a plate on which the car's serial number is stamped, usually located on the driver's-side door or on the top of the dashboard just behind the windshield.

IDLE—the speed at which the engine will sustain itself

smoothly with the transmission in neutral, while the car is stopped. On the typical engine it is 500 to 700 revolutions per minute of the crankshaft.

IDLER ARM—the part of the steering linkage that braces the linkage on the right side of the car.

IGNITION SYSTEM—the system that produces high-voltage electricity to create the spark at the spark plugs that fires the air-fuel mixture in the combustion chambers.

INTAKE MANIFOLD—a cast-metal part with passages to each intake port that channels the air-fuel mixture from the carburetor to the combustion chamber.

INTAKE PORT—a passage in the cylinder head that channels the air-fuel mixture flowing through the intake manifold into the combustion chamber when the intake valve opens.

INTAKE VALVE—the valve in the combustion chamber that opens to admit the air-fuel mixture.

L

LINKAGE—any system of rods, joints, pivots and other parts that transfers motion. Examples: gas pedal movement is transferred by linkage to a plate in the carburetor; gear shift lever movement is transferred by linkage to transmission gears.

LUBRICATION—the application of oil or grease to reduce friction.

M

MAGNETIC FIELD—an area of magnetic attraction that surrounds a magnet.

METERING VALVE—in a braking system with discs in front and drums in the rear, the metering valve delays the application of the disc brakes until the drum brakes' shoes have overcome the pressure of springs that hold them away from the drums. This provides balanced braking.

METRIC—the system of measurement used in all major countries except the United States and England. The basic unit of measurement is the meter (39.37 inches).

MODULATOR—a device threaded into the exterior of the automatic transmission and connected to the engine by a hose. The modulator informs the transmission of engine performance in order to aid the transmission's automatic shift decision-making process.

MUFFLER—the part of the exhaust system that reduces the sound produced by the flow of burned gases through the system.

N

NEEDLE AND SEAT VALVE ASSEMBLY—a valve in the carburetor that regulates the flow of fuel from the pump into the carburetor fuel bowl. It consists of a tapered needle that is pushed by a float into a seat to stop the flow of fuel.

NEUTRAL—the transmission gear position in which there is no transfer of power from the engine, allowing the engine to run while the car is stopped.

O

OIL FILTER (ENGINE)—a cannister with a filter inside that removes abrasive particles and contaminants from engine oil.

OIL FILTER (TRANSMISSION)—a filter that removes contaminants from transmission fluid.

OIL PAN—the bottom cover of the engine that stores oil not in use.

OIL PAN GASKET—a strip of material, usually cork or rubber, that seals the joint between the oil pan and the bottom of the engine block to prevent oil from leaking out.

OIL PUMP—the device that draws engine oil from the oil pan and pumps it to various parts of the engine to reduce friction.

OIL-THICKENING ADDITIVE—a product added to the engine oil to thicken it. On an older car, it may reduce oil consumption because thicker oil is less able to slip past worn piston rings into the combustion chamber.

OSCILLOSCOPE—an electronic tester with a televisionlike picture tube that is used by well-equipped shops to check ignition and charging systems.

OVERHAUL—to completely disassemble a component, clean all parts that can be reused, install new parts to replace those that are worn, and to reassemble the component.

P

PCV VALVE—a control valve that regulates the flow of gasoline vapors through the POSITIVE CRANKCASE VENTILATION system into the intake manifold.

PISTON—a close-fitting movable plug installed in a cylinder. When it is lowered, the cylinder can be filled with an air-fuel mixture. When it is pushed up, the mixture is compressed and ignited, forcing it down again. This downward force on the piston is power.

PISTON RING—a metal sealing ring fitted into a groove in the piston to improve its ability to seal the air-fuel mixture in the combustion chamber above it. The typical piston has three rings.

POSITIVE CRANKCASE VENTILATION (PCV)—a system of hoses and a valve that draw gasoline vapors that have slipped past the piston rings from the crankcase and channel them to the intake manifold, from where they flow into the combustion chambers.

POWER ASSIST—the general

term for any accessories that have a mechanism to make them easier to use. Engine-driven pumps are used to assist steering, vacuum diaphragms to assist braking, electric motors to move the windows, seats and radio antenna.

POWER BRAKES—a system which uses vacuum created in the engine to reduce the foot pedal pressure required to engage the brakes.

POWER STEERING—a steering system that uses oil under pressure to help move the steering linkage. The pressurized oil comes from a pump operated by a drive belt from the crankshaft pulley.

PRESSURE PLATE—the spring plate assembly that holds the clutch friction disc to the flywheel.

PULLEY—a "gear without teeth." Instead it has a groove in its circumference; a rubber belt tightly fitted in this groove transfers power to another such pulley.

PUSHROD—a long rod that is pushed upward by the valve lifter. The rod's upper end is in contact with one end of a pivoting part called a rocker, which it moves to open the valve.

R

RADIAL TIRE—a type of tire in which the rubber-impregnated fabric cords that form the carcass run across the tread area. These tires also have fabric or steel wire "belts" around the circumference to brace the tread.

RADIATOR—a finned, tubular assembly used in cars with a water-cooled engine, normally placed at the front of the engine compartment. The engine's water pump pushes hot coolant into the radiator, where the heat is passed into the atmosphere.

REAR AXLE ASSEMBLY—the assembly that changes the direction of the rotary motion of the driveshaft and transfers it to the rear wheels. Key components are a set of gears in the center and shafts which carry the power to the wheels.

REBUILT COMPONENT—a part that has been disassembled, refitted with new parts where necessary, cleaned and reassembled.

RECORE—a radiator whose finned main section has been replaced.

REFRIGERANT—the gas used in an air conditioning system. It has the property of boiling at minus 22 degrees F.

REMANUFACTURER — a producer of rebuilt components using an assembly-line process.

REPAIRS, LIGHT—this type of repair and maintenance work normally is featured by service stations. Typical jobs include replacing shock absorbers, mufflers, bulbs, filters, spark plugs, batteries and tires, plus lubrication, repair of flat tires and cooling system maintenance.

REPAIRS, MEDIUM—this type of repair work is done by some service stations and featured by garages. Typical jobs include brake work, fuel system and ignition system work (tune up), ball joints, springs, wheel alignment and balancing, charging and starting systems, air conditioning and engine service that can be done with the engine in the chassis.

REPAIRS, HEAVY—this type of repair work is normally done only by car dealers and garages, and in the case of garages, to a limited degree (some jobs in this category, but not all). Typical jobs include: replacing or overhauling transmission, engine, differential and steering box, and power window and power seat service.

RESISTOR—a device that restricts the flow of electricity.

RETREADED TIRES—used tire carcasses to which new treads have been bonded.

ROCKER ARM—a pivoting arm in the cylinder head that is moved by the pushrod to push open an intake or exhaust valve.

ROCKER COVER—see VALVE COVER.

ROLLER BEARING—a special type of bearing for a rotating part. It resembles the wheels on a rollerskate, mounted in a circular holder.

ROTARY MOTION—circular movement, as of a spinning wheel.

ROTOR—a key part of the ignition system. It sits on top of the distributor shaft, receives high-voltage electricity from the coil and transfers it to spark plug wires in the distributor cap.

RPM—engine speed in terms of *revolutions* of the crankshaft *per minute.* The typical engine can run without stalling at as low as 500 to 700 rpm, and develops its maximum power at 4500 to 5000 rpm.

S

SHOCK ABSORBER—a device filled with oil that stops the springs from flexing after they have absorbed the effects of an irregularity in the road.

SIGHT GLASS—a tiny window into the air conditioning system that permits checking for an adequate supply of refrigerant.

SOLENOID—a switch on the starter that allows all the current necessary to actuate the starter to flow to it from the battery.

SPARK PLUG—a unit with two electrical conductors called electrodes, that is threaded into a hole in the combustion chamber. High-voltage electricity from the ignition system travels down one electrode into the combustion chamber and jumps a small air gap to the second electrode, creating the spark that fires the air-fuel mixture. Each cylinder has one spark plug.

SPARK TIMING—the design factors in an ignition system that determine when the spark shall arrive at the spark plug to fire the air-fuel mixture in the

combustion chamber. A pair of reference marks, usually at the front of the engine, indicate when the spark timing is correct; if necessary, the mechanic can make an adjustment by slackening a clamp and slightly turning the body of the distributor. Automatic changes in spark timing, according to engine speed and load (acceleration or coasting), are made by the ignition system's vacuum and centrifugal advance devices.
STARTER—an electric motor with a gear that engages a gear on the flywheel.
STATOR—a component in the torque converter of an automatic transmission that directs oil flow for acceleration.
STEERING BOX—the housing that holds the gear at the end of the steering wheel shaft and the other gears that transfer motion from the steering wheel to the linkage that pivots the front wheels.
STEERING SYSTEM—the system that pivots the front wheels of the car to the left or

right. Turning the steering wheel turns a shaft with a gear at its other end. This gear sits in a housing with other gears, which convert the rotary motion into back-and-forth motion on an arm connected to the steering linkage.
SUSPENSION—the parts of the car that support the body: the springs, shock absorbers, control arms and ball joints.
SYNCHRONIZER—a part in a manual transmission that locks a gear onto a shaft.

T

TERMINAL (ELECTRICAL) —a specially shaped piece of metal attached to the end of a wire to facilitate connecting it.
THERMOSTAT—a temperature-sensitive device. In a water cooling system, a thermostat blocks the flow of water to the radiator until the engine has warmed up, thus speeding up the warmup process.

THERMOSTATIC AIR CLEANER—an air cleaner with a thermostat control that draws air into the engine from a duct on the exhaust manifold when the engine is cold. The use of heated air during engine warm-up improves performance and gas mileage, and reduces smog-forming exhaust emission.

THROTTLE PLATE—a circular plate in the carburetor air horn that is connected by cable and/or linkage to the gas pedal. Gas pedal movement pivots the plate to admit more air-fuel mixture into the engine.

TIMING CHAIN—a chain wrapped around the gears at the front of the crankshaft and camshaft that transfers power from the crankshaft to operate the camshaft.

TIMING COVER—a sheet metal cover at the front of the engine that covers the crankshaft and camshaft gears and the timing chain.

TIMING COVER GASKET— a strip of cork or rubber between the timing cover and the front of the engine that seals to prevent engine oil leakage at the joint.

TIMING LIGHT—a special tool that when properly connected to the ignition system flashes a light as the system delivers a spark to a plug. The light is aimed at reference marks, usually on the front of the engine. Every time the light goes on, the marks should be perfectly aligned. If they are not, the spark timing must be adjusted.

TORQUE CONVERTER—a device in front of the automatic transmission that performs the function of the manual transmission clutch. It consists of two fanlike parts, one bolted to the flywheel, the other attached to a shaft that goes into the transmission, in a circular cannister filled with oil. When the engine turns one part, the energy is transferred through oil movement to the other. A stator placed between the two "fans" directs the oil flow for maximum transfer of energy without complete transfer of speed; thus the engine fan can run faster than the transmission fan to provide good acceleration from a stopped position.

TRANSISTOR—an electronic device used in automobiles as a switch.

TREAD—the grooved portion of the tire that comes in contact with the road.

TUNEUP—a group of services and parts replacements performed on the ignition and fuel systems to restore performance. There is no standard set of included services but, in general, a tuneup includes service or replacement of spark plugs, condenser, ignition breaker points, air filter, gasoline filter, ignition timing and engine idle. It may also include cleaning and tightening of battery cable terminals, replacement of the PCV valve, tightening of cylinder-head-to-engine-block bolts, and valve adjustment.

V

V-8—an engine with eight cylinders arranged in two banks of four cylinders, each bank forming, in cross section, a leg of the letter V.

VACUUM ADVANCE—a device that pivots the plate on which the ignition breaker points are mounted to advance the times that the points open. Because the opening of the points creates the spark at the plugs, this action has the effect of advancing the spark timing. It consists of a rod attached to the plate and a diaphragm attached to the rod. A hose from the engine's intake manifold provides vacuum that, at the appropriate times, draws on the diaphragm, pulling it and the rod, and thus repositions the plate on which the points are mounted. The vacuum advance's action has the same effect as the CENTRIFUGAL ADVANCE, but it operates at a different time and provides a different amount of spark timing advance to meet different engine needs.

VALVE—a part that opens and closes a passage.

VALVE COVER—a sheet

metal cover on the top of the cylinder head (in a V-8 there are two covers, one for each side) that encloses the components of the valve train in the cylinder head.

VALVE COVER GASKET—a strip of cork or rubber between the valve cover and the top of the cylinder head that seals against oil leaks.

VALVE LIFTER—a cylindrical part that rests on the camshaft cams and moves up and down as the camshaft spins. It transfers motion to the pushrod which pivots the rocker to open a valve. Also see HYDRAULIC VALVE LIFTER.

VALVE SEAT—a surface against which a valve closes.

VALVE STEM—the round shank of the valve type used for intake and exhaust.

VAPOR LOCK—if the air in the engine compartment is very hot, the fuel in the pump and in the tubing may turn to vapor. Inasmuch as the carburetor bowl needs a supply of liquid fuel to mix with the inrushing air, it will starve for fuel and the engine will stall—a condition called vapor lock. Dousing the fuel pump and tubing with cold water may provide at least a temporary cure.

VOLTAGE REGULATOR—a device that controls the operation of the alternator or generator to keep it supplying the right amount of electricity to both operate the ignition system and electrical accessories and keep the battery charged.

W

WATER COOLING—the most widely used method of removing the excess heat of combustion from an engine. Water is pumped through passages in the cylinder head and block absorbs the heat, and then is pumped from the engine through the radiator, where it dissipates the heat into the air. The cooled water then flows back into the engine to again absorb and carry away heat.

WHEEL ALIGNMENT— measurement and correction (if necessary) of the angles of the front wheels and certain suspension parts with respect to the ground. The almost imperceptible angles by which these parts deviate from the straight up and down are important to normal handling, and special equipment is required to check these tiny deviations (called caster, camber and toe-in).

WHEEL CYLINDER (DRUM BRAKES)—a tiny cylinder containing two pistons, one near each end, mounted at each wheel. Brake fluid pumped under pressure from the brake master cylinder pushes each piston outward, which pushes brake shoe against the drum.